Real Estate Investing for Beginners

The Complete Step-by-Step Guide to Start Your Passive Income Business from the Plan to Finding a Deal with Real Estate Investment Tools and Tips

By Mark Prigun

TABLE OF CONTENTS

Introduction

Real estate investment includes the acquisition, ownership, management, rental, and sale of land for profit. Realty property improvements as a part of a real estate investment strategy are generally considered a sub-feature of land investment, such as land development. Land is a form of asset with limited liquidity relative to other assets. It is also capital intensive (although capital can also be obtained through mortgage leverage) and is very income dependent. If the investor does not understand and manage these factors well, the land becomes a risky investment.

Real estate markets in most countries are not organized or efficient for other, more liquid investment instruments. Individual properties are unique to themselves and are indirectly interchangeable, which presents a severe challenge for an investor seeking prices and investment opportunities. For this reason, properties that must take up space to locate may involve substantial work and competition among investors, with individual properties also being highly variable upon knowledge of availability. Information asymmetries are regular inland markets. This increases transaction risk, but also provides investors with many opportunities to acquire assets at bargain prices. Land entrepreneurs typically use a proliferation of valuation techniques to ascertain the value of properties before purchase.

Typical sources of investment properties include:

- Market listings (through a multiple listing service or commercial information exchange)

- Real estate agents and land brokers

- Banks (such as REOs and short-sale banks for land-owning departments)

- governmental entities (such as Federal National Mortgage Association, Federal Home Loan Mortgage Corporation, and other government agencies)

- Public auction (foreclosure sale, sale of the property)

- Crepitate sale (transaction by owner-buyer)

- Real estate wholesaler and investor (flipping)

Purchase of a listed stock investment is done, once the investment property is located, and the initial due diligence of checking and verifying the status of the situation completed. The investor will need to negotiate the purchase price and the terms of the sale with the seller, then execute a contract to purchase. . Most investors employ land agents and land lawyers to help in the acquisition process, as they are often quite complex, and improperly executed transactions are often costly. During the acquisition of a property, an investor will usually make a reasonable offer to make a purchase to pay "earnest money" to the seller for the deal, ordering the investor's rights to terminate the transaction at the beginning of the negotiation if price and conditions are not satisfactorily negotiated. This earnest may or may not be refundable and is considered to indicate the seriousness of the intent of the investor. The terms of the offer will typically include a variety of contingencies that allow the investor to cease diligence, inspect the property, and obtain financing among other requirements before the final purchase. Within the contingency period, the investor usually has the right to cancel the offer without penalty and to receive a return of earnest deposits. Once the contingency ends, the request is typically required to forfeit the earnest deposit upon resuming the proposal and must include other penalties.

Real estate assets are generally costly compared to other widely available investment instruments (such as stocks or bonds). Only rarely will land investors pay the entire amount of the property's acquisition price in cash. Typically, a large portion of the acquisition value can be financed using financial instruments or loans, such as the collateral of a real estate loan by the property. The amount of acquisition value financed by debt is called leverage. The amounts funded by the investor's capital through cash or other asset transfers are referred to as equity. The leverage ratio of the total estimated value (often referred to as "LTV" or loan to a standard mortgage) is a mathematical measure of the risk an investor is taking to finance the acquisition of a property. Investors typically seek to reduce their equity requirements and increase their leverage, so that their return on investment (ROI) is maximized. Lenders and other financial institutions usually have minimum equity requirements for the land investment they are asked to finance, generally on the order of 20% of the appraised value. Investors looking for lower equity requirements may explore alternative financing arrangements as part of the acquisition of the property (e.g., seller financing, seller subordination, private equity sources).

If the property required repairs

If the property required repairments, then traditional lenders like banks will often not lend on such a property, and so the investor has a hard lender. Hard money loans may require borrowing from a personal lender, like a short-term bridge loan. Hard money loans are usually short-term loans where the lender charges a higher rate of interest due to the upside risk nature of the loan. Hard money loans are generally at a lower loan-to-value ratio than traditional mortgages.

Some land investment organizations, such as the Land Investment Trust (REIT) and some pension funds and hedge funds, have ample capital reserves and investment strategies, which allow 100% equity in the purchase of those assets. This reduces the risk that levitation brings, but also limits potential ROI.

By taking advantage of the acquisition of an investment property, specified periodic payments to service the debt create ongoing (and sometimes large) negative income from the time of purchase. This is sometimes mentioned because of the carrying cost or "carry" of the investment. Land investors must manage their cash flow to minimize enough positive income from the property to offset carrying costs to achieve success.

Net operating income, or NOI, is the sum of all positive cash derived from rent and other sources of ordinary income generated from an asset, the sum of ongoing expenses, such as maintenance, utilities, fees, taxes, and others. Nature (Debt service is not a fact in NOI). The ratio of NOI is expressed as a percentage, as the value of the asset, is called the capitalization rate or the CAP rate, and can be a general measure of the performance of an investment asset.

Tax shelter offsets occur in one of three ways: depreciation (which can sometimes be accelerated), tax credits, and carryover losses that reduce liabilities levied against income from other sources for a period of 27.5 years. Some asylum benefits are often transferable, counting the laws governing liabilities within the jurisdiction where the assets are found. These are often sold to others for cash returns or other profit.

Equity build-up is an increase within the investor's equity ratio, as the portion of debt service payments devoted to principal funds over time. Equity build-up is counted as a positive income from an asset where remuneration is paid from the support rather than from independent income sources.

The appreciation of capital is the increase in the market value of an asset over time, realized as income when the asset is sold. Unless it is part of a strategy for growth and improvement, capital appreciation is very unpredictable. The purchase of an asset in which large portions of projected cash flow is expected from capital appreciation (price increases) rather than from other sources is taken into speculative rather than investment.

Some individuals and corporations have focused their investment strategy to purchase properties that are in some stage of foreclosure. A property is taken into consideration in pre-foreclosure when the homeowner has defaulted on their real estate loan. The formal foreclosure process varies by state and must be judicial or non-judicial, affecting the length of time your property is within the pre-foreclosure phase. Once the legal foreclosure process is underway, these properties are often purchased at a public sale, commonly called a foreclosure auction or execution sale. If the property is not sold at the auction to the general public, ownership of the property is returned to the lender. The properties of this phase are called the owner of the land, or REO.

Once a property is sold in a foreclosure auction or as an REO, lenders can keep the proceeds to satisfy their mortgage and any legal costs they deducted from selling prices and any outstanding tax obligations.

During the REO phase, the foreclosing bank or financial institution still has the right to honor tenant leases (if there are tenants within the property). Still, the bank usually wants to vacate the property so that it can sell more easily.

Buy, rehab, rent, refinance (BRRR) can be a land investment strategy, employed by land investors who have experience renovating or rehabilitating properties, but who consistently own a place in a rental property for income. Some investors add another R which stands for Repeat as a real estate portfolio is built.

A real estate investor buys an investment property with a depressed value because it needs repairs and cosmetic updates. The investor then updates the property, including the structural repairs required to bring a house up to the current code.

This often includes cosmetic updates such as new paint, flooring, tiles, countertops, and kitchen appliances.

The investor then finds a tenant and acquires the landlord, which is usually every month. The property is refinanced again, generally for a fully amortized 30-year loan.

It clearly cannot fall under the category of "real estate investment," although it is worth noting. Each state creates systems and rules for the lien or deed process. Careful research is essential. Typically, property owners are informed of the amount of taxes owed and given a period to pay you. If the quantity remains lacking, the state will take one of the latter paths (though some have created a hybrid). Tax Lien state

Tax lien state is the county during which the property is found, selling the lien certificate in a purchase or auction. Some states sell the lien for the outstanding amount, while others allow bidding. The buyer of the lien collects interest (predetermined) from the owner of the house on the amount that was purchased. If the lien becomes unpaid (with interest) during the redemption period, the investor can freeze the house. Unlike most foreclosures, when a lien is considered, all other liars and mortgages are terminated, and the property will, therefore, be "free and clear." Lenders can usually pay a lien to avoid losing their homes and property.

Tax Deed The state

The county government sells the deed to the property at a public sale or auction. The advantage for investors is the ability to acquire property at discounted rates, often for outstanding amounts in taxes. When an account becomes delinquent, the property is listed in the tax assessor's office, some also online. Investors usually purchase properties with homes before foreclosure (often referred to as sharks).

CHAPTER 1
Identify your financial phase

The world of land investment is, in general, crammed with special stages that can be very intimidating. While you do not need to be an expert in every field, you should know several essential steps required to avoid any complication. Instead of trying to read every investment book, try to get a working knowledge of the different stages of investing in land. If you are not focusing on them all at once and using up only one or two things, then over time, the business will not be nearly as difficult. Below are several of the most important phases of the critical property industry:

1.) Buying

Buying a house deals with two essential but different areas: making an offer and getting a mortgage. Even though they are both independent, if one is not completed, then the deal cannot progress.. While working closely with a realtor, one of the primary things that will be discussed is commission. This is often merely the quantity you pay them to search for a property, present your offer, and follow up with any item that comes up during the method. Once you are interested, they are going to ask you for an earnest money deposit (EMD), which will be with the broker if your proposal is accepted. They are also going to ask for a pre-payment letter from a lender.

2.) Financing

Stage Two can also be referred to as Stage 1A; you must promote before you meet a realtor. The didactic process is simply the action of a lender or broker to review your credit, income, and assets to verify what is approved. You will hear terms like credit score, debt-to-income ratio, private mortgage insurance, and loan to value. Your debt-to-income balance involves adding all minimum payments on any loan and dividing that number into your gross monthly income. If you got a replica of your credit report and a mortgage calculator app, you would easily get this number. Private mortgage insurance (PMI) is a monthly fee that your lender charges if you set 20% on your mortgage. It is often a type of implied insurance against foreclosure and default. In the end, the loan to your value is the loan amount against the value or selling price of your property. The more you set, the lower the number. If you set above 20% or 80%, you will be subject to non-public mortgage insurance.

3.) After closing

On the day of closing, you will do another set of terms and phrases. Much of the closing information is stated to be a description of the settlement of HUD-1, otherwise known as HUD. By law, you will see it before it is shown at the final sale, so you will have some time to review it. In this document, you will see where all your money goes. You will see the exact mortgage closing costs, attorney fees, prepaid land tax amount, and any credit from the seller. Take time to read through this document (one page and two-sided). If you have any questions, run them by your lawyer along with your realtor. You will notice any deposit made, where each dollar is headed within the transaction. It is good practice to review your HUD, even if to help you assess closing costs.

4.) Rehab

If you choose to rehab or flip your property, there will be another set of terms, phrases, and lingo to spread. If you are working, most of them should be familiar. If not, the primary thing you want to do is to walk around the property with a notebook and write down everything you are not entirely comfortable with. Between oil tanks, fuse boxes, furnaces, room dimensions, and window types, many things structure an asset - each of which has a dedicated vocabulary. From there, conduct your research. You will do much legwork yourself or ask as many questions as you want, working with you. What you want to achieve is to think about what some items are worth, what they are doing, and what they are called. This is a part of the method in which it takes many deals to get comfortable.

Not knowing about these steps is not an excuse for not knowing. Like in almost everything, you will learn tons more by waiting onshore. If you have got some downtime, open an investment book, or attend one of the various websites and skim about your craft. The more you recognize, the more confident you will be. There is much information at every stage of the critical property business. If you consider one area at a time, you will specialize in time.

Project finance is the long-term financing of independent capital investment, projects with cash flows, and assets that will be identified separately.

Land project finance can be an excellent example. Other samples of project finance include mining, oil and gas, and buildings and construction.

Real estate project finance cash flow should be enough to hide operating expenses and fund financing repayment requirements. Typically, financing is formed from debt and equity that corresponds to the asset's lifetime.

Real Estate Project Finance vs. Finance

When an organization takes a replacement investment, it can use cash flow from other operating activities to fund a new project. It can also use its regular credit to borrow money and support the project. The corporation may issue equity with an indefinite horizon. In land project finance, the equity habitual to fund the project is usually repaid on top of the selected time horizon.

Pile of capital in land project finance

When it involves land project finance, the capital pile includes several considerations, as follows:

• Drawing on construction loans for financing.

- Security and priority for various lenders within the capital cycle.

- For the development and sale of the project, and that corresponds to the length of your time.

- A value between the fixed and floating rate of interest Marketing.

- Equity.

The capital stack, which includes all types of financing that will be used, typically consists of the following:

- Senior debt

- Subordinated debt

- Equity

Senior debt is the most secure capital, while equity is the least risky of the three.

Terms and Definitions of the Real Estate Project Finance Industry

To build a financial model, we must know the essential terms and definitions often used in land project finance:

- Loan to Value (LTV): the amount of loan to a lender. Percentage of the market value of the critical asset.

- Loan for Cost (LTC): The amount of lending the lender will provide as a percentage of the price of development.

- Cap Rate: NOI divided by the value of the asset, expressed as a percentage.

- Amortization Period: The period (month or year) the original repayment of a loan fancy must be completed.

- General Partner (GP): An owner of a partnership with unlimited liability - usually a manager who actively participates within operations.

- Limited Partner (LP): A passive investor who has limited capacity, supported the amount to be invested within the project.

- Land loan: Financing. No one wants to acquire a little bit of land with NOI. Long-term values are going to be much lower than income-producing assets.

- Floor Space Ratio (FSR): used to determine the dimensions of a building and control the density of development on a parcel of land.

• Gross Building Area (GBA): The sum of all construction sites from wall to wall.

• Gross Area Payable (GLA): The amount of all enclosed space.

• Gross Site Area: Two-dimensional measurements of a site support its property lines.

• Net Site Area: Gross Site Area, Reduction.

• Max GBA: Calculates gross building area, supports FSR.

• Construction GBA: The Gross building sector supports construction plans.

• Salable Area: Aggregated construction area supported construction, less common space, or other non-salable areas.

CHAPTER 2
Target market

An audience is the target group or reader for a publication, advertisement, or other messages. In marketing and advertising; it is a specific group of consumers within a predetermined target market, identified as the target or recipient for a particular advertisement or message. Businesses that have a good target market will certainly specialize in sending messages to selected audiences, such as advertisements for The Body Shops Mother's Day, aimed at girls' partners rather than the entire market, perhaps women were also involved.

An audience is created by a similar factor as the target market but is more specific and vulnerable to being influenced by other factors. An example of this was the marketing of USDA's Food Guide, which was intended to appeal to children between two and eighteen years old. Factors that had to be considered outside of the quality marketing mix included the nutritional needs of growing children, children's knowledge and attitudes about nutrition, and other specifics. This reduced their target market and provided expertise to select audiences. General factors for the target audience may reduce the target market for specific people such as' men aged 20–30 who live in Auckland, New Zealand rather than men aged 20–30'. However, just because an audience is specific does not suggest that the message being delivered will not be of interest and will not be received outside the intended demographic. Failure to target the selected audience is also possible and occurs when information is misreported. Campaign backfires, and side effects like 'demerit goodies' are expected results of a failed drive. Demerit goods are goods with a negative social perception, and the consequences of their image counteract against commonly accepted social values.

Defining the difference between a target market and an audience falls just below the difference between marketing and advertising. In marketing, a call is targeted by business strategies, while television shows, music, and media, such as advertising and media, seek to attract audiences more effectively. One possible strategy to appeal to the audience would be to advertise toys during children's TV programs in the morning instead of in the evening.

A target market can be a select group of potential or current consumers, a business that targets its marketing and advertising strategies to sell its product and service. Defining the 'target market' is the first step within the marketing strategy of a business and can be a process of market segmentation. Market segmentation is often defined as the market divided into select groups, supporting the proliferation of such things as needs, characteristics, and behaviors, so that the tools of the marketing mix are often appropriate for the individual. Market segmentation empowers a business to define its target market for its product or service and implement the marketing mix to realize the specified results.

Demographic information

Demographic information includes statistical aspects of consumers such as gender, ethnicity, income, qualifications, and legal status. Demographic information is essential to the business because it gives a necessary background to the buyers whose business aims to target their marketing campaign. This helps them communicate effectively at a basic level with which they need to be recognized by the audience. Demographics are essential because they supply the motivation that the business is going to target. Demography is statistical information that does not require in-depth analysis to supply solutions. Thus, a business will use quantitative methods of knowledge collection. This short method will provide a statistical approach to identify audiences.

Information

Psychological psychiatry is the use of sociological, psychological, and anthropological factors, as well as consumer behavior, to survive and self-conceptualize how different market segment groups make decisions, certain philosophies, individuals, or products. Psychological information is often used by people involved in business to gain a deeper understanding of the buyer groups used by the business through the analysis of more intimate details of the consumer's lifestyle and thinking processes. Things like financials, interests, hobbies, and lifestyles will all be filtered by the business to create an audience that will, in theory, be hospitable to goods and can connect to the business through a marketing campaign.

Behavioral information

Consumer behavior is the purchase decision process, which affects consumers' purchasing decisions, for what purpose they use the purchased goods and their responses and attitudes to the goods.

Cheng et al. (20029), explains that consumer behavior is plagued by messages sent by businesses, which successfully influence their attitudes towards brands and products, and ultimately what products they want to buy. When determining its audience, a business must examine consumer behavior trends. Behavioral trends may include online shopping rather than in-store shopping, or modern consumers may purchase a replacement smartphone annually. They should then select a segment of consumers whose behavior aligns with the functionality and purpose of the goods as the target audience for the marketing campaign. Businesses often identify target consumers because they are going to indicate that by their behavioral cues, there is a need for merchants. Their interests, hobbies, and past purchasing activity provide a platform on which businesses can base their marketing campaigns.

Geographical information

Geographical information is where the customer is found and is essential to the business once they determine their audience. This often happens because customers located in multiple geographies are faced with various things that influence their purchasing decisions. These are often many things, inclusive of resources, cultures, and climate, which can cause their behavior, psychological information, and influences to vary with those who are in the same demographic but are geographically far away. For example, a city or region with a significant drinking culture will face high alcohol sales. In contrast, a city or region with a minimal drinking culture will experience low alcohol sales. Each country has consumers of a similar demographic, but thanks to the cultural influence of the geographic region, their purchasing decisions are different.

A basic example of a consumer profile is: men aged 35–40, who sleep in the US and have university-level education (demographic), are sociopolitical extroverts from a top-middle economic class and have a vibrant lifestyle (psychological); lives in Nashville, Tennessee (geographic) and makes small and frequent purchases without considering the product's brand (behavior). This profile will allow the business to attract its marketing campaign to specific consumers.

There are several methods of demographic, psychological, geographic, and behavioral data collection. There are quantitative methods, statistical procedures like surveys and questionnaires, and qualitative methods, in-depth approaches such as focus groups or extensive interviews. Different aspects of consumers are essential to the business when planning a marketing campaign, as the information the business collects will determine what the profitable target market for the campaign is, and how to succeed in this market.

Businesses will also have to watch their competitors to find out what process they are currently adopting and resolve the case, and which consumers they are targeting. This can give the business an opportunity to think about the type of consumer they are going to target, and what is the simplest way to talk with such a consumer. This information is often used to allow the business to be slightly differentiated from the competition to provide them with a competitive advantage once the marketing campaign is launched.

Once the audience is identified, the business must create content for the campaign that resonates and effectively communicates with the buyer. TRAI Sherlock emphasizes that the content with which the business is about to reach the buyer must be high quality, as 92% of marketers specify that high-level content is effective for a campaign. This high level of coverage will help consumers connect with the business on a more personal level and contribute to a successful communication process from the business to the audience, then get feedback from the audience for the business.

Once a business has collected data from consumers about their demographic, psychological, geographic, and behavioral conditions, they will analyze it and use it to show the audience broadly. This will be refined by analysis of competitors' processes and goals, allowing the business to create a more fragmented audience. Then the fragmented audience is often distilled into a transparent objective, whereby consumers target the business, thus making the exact audience for a marketing campaign.

Reaching an audience can be a staging process, starting with the world's choice of the target market. A successful appeal to the audience requires an intensive media plan, which includes many factors to realize an efficient campaign.

The use of media distinguishes the target market from the target audience. While target markets are marketed with business strategies, advertising, and other media tools are used to focus on the audience in a simple way to appeal to a group of people. The effectiveness of an audience campaign depends on how well the corporate knows its market; it will include details such as behavior, incentives, cultural differences, and social expectations. Failure to achieve these trends can lead to campaigns being targeted at the wrong audience, and ultimately a loss of cash or at least no change. An example of such a failure was Chef Board, who planned a campaign to appeal to teenage boys, the most critical consumers of their product. However, they did not notice that the buyers of their goods could also be different from the consumers, which was the case, as the mothers were the leading buyers, although the boys were consuming the goods. Factors such as these are considered at a greater depth level with depth media planning, which cannot be found during a simple target market strategy.

Through media planning, every step requires attention, and different types of factors need to be considered. These include:

- Target

- Media Type

- Media Strategy

- Media Vehicles

- Media Units

- Media Schedules

- Media Promotions

- Media Logistics

- Contingency Planning

- Calendar

Budgets and Integrated Marketing

Each of those sections goes into even greater detail like media units, and such minutes Include details of the length of a broadcast advertisement or the dimensions of a print advertisement.

Achieving outright success during a campaign requires a fully followed, planned, and implemented media plan. Therefore, ignoring any factor can lead to miscommunication with consumers and, ultimately, a failure to reach the entire audience effectively.

Effective marketing identifies an acceptable audience and can employ the right marketing strategy to succeed and influence them. There are four major targeting strategies mainly used in businesses; undivided (mass) marketing, differentiated (segment) marketing, focused (niche) marketing, and finally micro (local or personal) marketing.

Crude (mass) marketing can be a strategy to capture an entire audience, rather than specialize in segmented markets. A business will typically design a line and most often specialize in consumer demand, to create a marketing program that will appeal to the best amount of shopping. This strategy typically uses mass distribution and advertising to help create an appreciable product and is probably one of the most important, and cost-effective. Narrow lines, entire advertising programs, and the absence of segment marketing research and planning all contribute to keeping prices down. Many do not believe in this strategy, thanks to the high amount of competition and, therefore, the difficulty of creating a product that satisfies most consumers.

A differentiated (segmented) marketing strategy is when a business chooses to focus on multiple segments of the audience, creating a variety of its product for each. An example of this is often the V Energy drink, which offers an external range of products; V regular, v sugar-free, v zero, v double espresso (v-energy., ND). While typically using this marketing strategy, corporate recognition is widened, and repeat purchases are strengthened; customers receive products that fit their needs. This strategy is, unfortunately, not effective and involves tons of research and development, as well as a full range of promotions that are unique to each specific product. However, this strategy often leads to more sales than those who do not use the marketing strategy. When considering this strategy, one must consider the increased sales against the increased costs.

Focused (niche) marketing can be a "market coverage strategy, during which a corporation goes after an outlier of 1 or two sub-markets." This strategy enables companies to create a strong market position without production, distribution, or advertising. This strategy is generally beneficial as it does not involve tons of competition. A business can realize more and more knowledge of its separate segment, as they focus more on the needs and reputation of the division that achieves this. Many companies using this strategy are now turning to online to make them shop online, not only because it is effective, but it also allows them to be more recognizable.

A micro-marketing strategy (local or individual) targets far less than an uncertain marketing strategy. Typically, a business using this strategy will adjust its product and marketing program to suit the needs of different market segments and niches. This is frequently shown within the real estate industry, which often aims to work out what kind of home a customer is trying to find. Micro-marketing involves both local and personal marketing. This strategy is oftentimes more expensive, thanks to the optimization and lack of economies of scale.

Sales have particular difficulties when it involves manufacturing and marketing costs, which meet various requirements for every marketplace and brand image familiarity—new development technologies and fragmented markets overcome these barriers regularly.

The businessmen in marketing to specify individual marketing refers to adjusting events to individual customer demand. An example of this is often Coca-Cola, which enables customers to personalize their Coke cans, having the ability to print their name or choice of text on the packaging. It allows customers to style and create a product that they want to suit their needs, creating value and loyalty for the business, despite additional costs for the establishment, also how the business can stack up against its rivals.

Marketers have outlined four basic strategies to satisfy target markets: undivided marketing or mass marketing, differentiated marketing, focused marketing, and micro marketing/niche marketing.

Mass marketing can be a market coverage strategy, during which a firm ignores market segment differences and follows the entire market with an offer. It is the marketing of a product (or an effort to sell through persuasion) to a good audience. The idea is to broadcast a message that will reach the most significant number of possible individuals. Traditionally mass marketing has focused on radio, television, and newspapers as the medium is attuned to reach this broad audience.

For sales teams, one way to succeed in the target market is through marketing. This is often done by purchasing consumer databases that support partition profiles that you define. These databases usually come with consumer contacts.

Caution is suggested when making marketing efforts - check the marketing laws of the targeted country.

Target audiences are formed from different groups, for example, adults, teens, children, mid-teens, preschoolers, men, or women.

To effectively market to any given audience, it is necessary to be conversational to your target market; their habits, behaviors, likes, and dislikes. Needs vary within the size, classification, geographic scale, locality, types of communities, and different types of sales. The different variations involved during a deal are essential, as you cannot adjust everyone's preferences to understand whom you are marketing.

To become better acquainted with the ins and outs of the legend of its designated target market, one must complete marketing research. Marketing research can be a documented examination of a market that wants to know business preparation activities for inventory, procurement, workforce expansion/contraction, facility expansion, capital equipment procurement, promotional activities, improvement of daily tasks, and other aspects.

Mass marketing (undivided marketing)

Undefined marketing/mass marketing can be a method that many of us employ to focus as much as possible on advertising a message that marketers understand the target market (Ramya and Subasi). When television first surfaced, undivided marketing was used in most commercial campaigns to spread a message to a group of individuals. Over the past few years, the types of commercials that have been played on TV are often similar to each other in an attempt to make the audience laugh; these same ads will play on air for many viewers or viewers who will focus on more and more viewers. One of the positive aspects of undivided marketing. However, there are also negative aspects to mass marketing because not everyone thinks about the same, so it can be complicated to urge a message equal to a vast number of individuals (Ramya and Up shakti).

Differentiated marketing strategy

Differentiated marketing can be a practice, during which different messages are advertised to appeal to certain groups of individuals within the target market (Ramya and Sub shakti). Differentiated marketing, however, can be a method that requires a tug of cash. Whenever messages are being converted to advertise different messages, it is costly to try to do this because it costs whenever a piece of information is in the market. Differentiated marketing also requires a lot of time and energy because it takes time to return with ideas and presentations to plug in different messages; using this method also involves many resources. But all the time, investing money and resources in different marketing is often worthwhile when it comes to the right because different messages can successfully reach the target group of individuals and successfully target those messages to those targeted groups of individuals. May inspire us to follow what Ramya and Ramayana are doing. Hamasaki).

Focused marketing or niche marketing is a term used in niche marketing business that focuses solely on selling its products and services to a selected target market. Despite being attractive to small businesses, niche marketing is a challenging marketing strategy because companies can do intensive and thorough research to succeed in their specific target market to be successful.

Niche marketing is when a firm or company focuses on a specific aspect or group of consumers to deliver its product and marketing. Niche marketing additionally referred to as concentrated marketing, suggests that firms are using all their resources and skills in a place. Niche marketing has become one of the most successful marketing strategies for many firms because it identifies vital resources and provides the marketer with a selected category, in which to convey and present information to the expert. This enables companies to gain a competitive advantage over other large companies targeting the equivalent group; as a result, it generates higher profit margins. Smaller companies usually implement this method, so that they are ready to consider an aspect and give full priority, enabling them to compete with larger companies.

Some features of niche marketing help the marketing team determine marketing schedules and supply clear and specific establishments for marketing plans and goal setting. Typically, niche marketing naturally occurs when companies react to the current situation.

There are alternative methods for firms to spot their niche market, but the most common technique applied to locate a different segment is to employ a marketing audit. This is often the case where a firm evaluates several internal and external factors. Factors implemented within the audit identify the company's weaknesses and strengths, the company's current customer base, and modern marketing techniques. It is then able to determine which marketing approach would be most appropriate in their niche.

There are five key aspects or steps that are required to realize successful niche marketing. These five steps include:

1. : Developing a marketing plan

2. : Focusing on your marketing program

3. Niche to compete against big companies

4. Niche based on expertise

5. Developing cavities through mergers

Developing a marketing plan:

Developing a market plan is when a firm's marketing team evaluates the current state of the firm, with focus on the potential and any potential competition for the corporation. A market plan may include elements such as target market, consumer interest, and resources. It should be distinct and the dominant group of consumers as it is a specialty of niche marketing.

Focus on your marketing program:

Focusing your marketing program is when employees are using marketing tools and skills to improve their capabilities to raise market awareness for the corporate. Niche marketing is not only used to stay at a competitive advantage within the industry. Still, it is additionally used to learn how to attract more consumers and grow your customer database.

Using these skills, the corporate is then ready to implement its strategy consistently.

Niche to Compete against Large Firms:

Small and medium-sized companies are ready to compete against niche marketing, as they are prepared to specialize in a primary niche, which helps the cavity to grow. Small firms can investigate the problems of their customers within their niche and then provide different marketing to appeal to consumer interest.

Niche based on expertise:

When new companies are formed, different people bring different types of experiences to the corporate. This is often another type of niche marketing, referred to as niche-backed expertise, where individuals with tons of experience during a specific niche can continue to market for that niche because they know that the cavity is part of corporate Will give positive results for

Development of niches through mergers:

A company may have found its potential niche but are unable to plug its product or service across the cavity. This is often where experts from the merger industry are used. Together the company may have the tools and skills to plug into the recess, and therefore, others may have the talent to gather all the necessary information needed to conduct this marketing. Conforming to niche marketing, if done effectively, is often an immensely powerful concept.

Overall, niche marketing can be a great marketing strategy for companies, mainly small and medium-sized firms, as it can be a specialized and easy marketing approach. Once a firm's niche is identified, a team of marketers can implement relevant marketing to meet the desires and demands of that niche.

Niche marketing is also strongly associated with marketing because marketing can be easily implemented within target markets thanks to a simple marketing approach.

Direct marketing

Direct marketing can be a method that firms are ready to market to their customers' needs and needs; it focuses on consumer spending habits and their potential interests. Firms use marketing as a channel to interact and reach their existing consumers. Marketing is accomplished by collecting consumer data in various ways. An example is Internet and social media platforms such as Facebook, Twitter, and Snapchat. They are a duo of online methods that allow organizations to understand what their consumers like and gather their data to enable organizations to cater to their target markets and their interest. This method of selling is becoming increasingly popular as data will allow organizations to come back with simpler promotional strategies and is available with better customized promotional offers that buyers find accurate, it will enable organizations to use their resources more. It will also allow them to do so effectively and efficiently, and improve customer management relationships. A vital tool organization use in marketing is the RFM model (repetition-frequency-monetary value). Despite all the benefits this method can bring, it is often costly, suggesting that organizations with low budget constraints will have trouble using this method of selling.

When it involves property, the dream of every seller to make a successful sale. However, to try to do this, it is essential to plug your property according to the right market which can be broadly classified into six primary segments: entry-level buyer, family buyer, the mature or second-time buyer, holiday, investment buyers and high-end buyers.

Entry-level buyer

South Africa areas rank high on the agenda of ownership of the property and open market are the steps to do an outer part of the structure of the market, especially for first-time buyers. It is essential to keep in mind that if you are marketing your property in the current segment, many buyers will have limited budgets, want real value for money, and possibly have a hard conversation to urge what they want.

Family

Family-oriented buyers have particular requirements when it involves purchasing a home. Decision-making factors for these buyers usually include proximity to good schools and every necessary facility like hospitals. Family home buyers search for safe properties where their children can grow up in safety but also earn an honest return on their property when their children leave the nest. Other decisive factors for such buyers include price advertising such as swimming baths, a large garden, and an entertainment area.

Mature buyers

Alive longer so is the demand for properties that cater to the current segment. Mature buyers at or near retirement age require certain characteristics that are non-negotiable. These include single-story residences and well-proportioned bathrooms such as handrails and emergency buttons. Security is additionally a significant concern for such buyers. Homes for mature buyers will inevitably be on the verge of medical facilities.

Holiday Buyers

Vacation shoppers generally seek vacation or second homes that are easily accessible, on the verge of many attractions, easy to care for, and secure. If you feel that your home falls in this category and you need to attract buyers during this segment, then be sure to consider these points.

Investment Buyers: During

In this section, buyers usually purchase property intending to lease it. For these buyers, this type of buying does not support sentiment but is generally driven by data on investment returns. In other words, for a property to appeal to an investment buyer, it must show potential for both capital appreciation and income.

To an extent, investment buyers should be knowledgeable about the property as it involves risks and expenses. For example, one of the hazards is the ability to seek suitable tenants for the investment buyer. There are also tax implications that need to be considered. As such, these sellers must do their homework on these aspects if they hope to attract investment buyers.

High-end buyers for many buyers, the 'right' address is incredibly important. Distinctive features such as superior end-suite bathrooms and high-end fixtures and finishes are also essential considerations for these buyers. Good safety and proximity to major arterial routes, including critical business nodes, are all aspects that stand out as equally crucial during this market decision and will be factored according to your marketing plan.

General Guidelines:

Although various factors apply to different buyers, some general rules apply to all or any properties.

• First impressions ultimately become an essential part of the outside of your property.

• Confirm that the property is clean, unused and well maintained

• Keep your property ready. Buyers will feel a lot more positive about some potential purchases if any cosmetic or structural issues have already been addressed

• Commission an honest agent who will help facilitate a fast, successful sale and make life just a touch easier for all concerned.

CHAPTER 3
The location of the property

To purchase an investment property involves thorough research and evaluation. You want to give yourself the easiest opportunity to make an honest investment. Here are four criteria that you should check before purchasing your next rental property.

The location of the property is essential.

You cannot change the position of a property, so it is one of the most important things when evaluating a potential investment. For example, a university has several benefits of shopping for an income property. The idea is that new students will always have to try to find accommodation, parents of students often pay rent, and you will often recover better rent due to the desirability of the world and the increasing demand for apartments.

Location characteristics to consider are urban, suburban, or rural? How far are the requirements such as grocery stores, shopping, transportation, schools, and hospitals?

Imagine the type of tenant who wants to measure their families, superiors, single people, capitalists. Is there a high demand for rentals within the area? How appropriate is it from your primary residence? - If it is far away, then you must think about the cost of travel and the opportunity cost from lost productivity. Is the neighborhood stable, expanding, or declining? - Are there tons of vacant property or tons of latest construction?

Do you get a chance for development within the future? - For example, a replacement railway that connects to a severe city is being built, or a replacement company is relocating the world and creating new jobs. These can dramatically increase the desirability of the situation.

Run the numbers to know your budget. Consider the following:

- How much money can you invest in this investment?

- How much are you willing to lose?

- If you want additional funds, where will you get them?

- How much would you like to borrow? - What will be your monthly mortgage payment and interest rate?

Determine the value of the property:

- Request a particular income and expense sheet for the property. If none are available, confirm that you are ready to make a reasonable estimate of operating costs.

- Compute the Internet Operating Income (NOI) for the asset.

- What is the quality percentage for your area?

- What is the approximate rent for the property?

- What will be the insurance cost?

- How much are the taxes?

- What will be the annual property maintenance cost?

- Have you set the capitalization rate (cap rate) of your market? If you are unaware of your market cap rate, an area land broker can usually provide this information.

- Once you have set the cap rate, you will now divide the NOI by the cap rate and get the present value of the asset.

- Have you done comparative marketing research (CMA)?

- Were you selling for comparable homes within this area? Whether you are buying a rental property or want to flip the house, you will want to make sure that you do not pay more for the property.

- Make a list of necessary repairs that you are comfortable with.

If you need a property that needs cosmetic repairs just like a coat of paint and new carpet, then you are comfortable with a generous amount of labor, or you have someone carrying new plumbing, electrical, flooring, walls, are comfortable with rehab).

Do you affect the necessary repair?

The cost of repair will vary significantly if you are ready to roll yourself into the grass or if you want to hire someone else to try it.

The cost of labor is higher in some parts of the country than in others.

The cost of materials depends on the value of the property. You will need higher quality materials for a property of $ 1,000,000 compared to a fifty thousand dollars one.

It will always cost a lot to repair. The budget and estimated time of completion are often double. Not only will you pay more for special repairs, but you will pay additional financing costs, called "soft costs," to pay mortgage property, taxes, and insurance on the vacant property while these additional repairs are completed.

Understand the current land market

Trying to flip McMaster during a downturn will not be the simplest undertaking. During a recession, purchasing a foreclosed property to rent to tenants may be a better bet for fulfillment. If you shop for that Mm expansion and have the cash to carry it for seven years, if you sell it for a profit, then yes, it could be an honest investment. Are you looking to market and sell quickly, or are you planning for a long-term holding strategy?

Another thing to note while purchasing the property is its resale value. Highly desirable assets are those that are often easily bought and sold, no matter the market. They are always in demand. Like bread and water, consider them necessary.

People do not need a home with a cluttered pool and television screening room. People need a house with a clean bathroom and a strong roof. You want your property to appeal to the best number of individuals so that you get the best number of potential tenants and buyers.

Location and Price

Like a stock on an exchange, a house has a price that fluctuates. The value of the land supports the initial cost of a home at the time of purchase, the value of the construction of the house, and the percentage of markup for profit to the builder.

Land and residential value then rise and fall with properties around it and, therefore, commercial or recreational activities developing nearby. Several factors can affect the price of a home, but one of the most influential in the area.

Value is an elusive concept - something that is valuable to at least one person may not be to someone else. The price of the land may vary slightly, with the houses having a rough market value supporting the dimensions of the house, the dimensions of the lot, when it was built, and of course, the location.

Locations with high value

Home values are driven by supply and demand. When there is more demand for homes, but insufficient supply, house prices rise. Why are some places higher than others? Some places are in demand because:

- People with children are concerned about their children's education, and sometimes they can pay more for a home that has high test scores and an honest reputation as an administrative district.

- Homes, rivers, lakes, or parks near the sea deserve higher home values thanks to good views and outdoor recreation opportunities.

- Some places sell quickly and for top dollar because they provide comprehensive views of the cityscape. Even a glimpse of the ocean from a window is enough to authenticate an upright location. Other in-demand ideas include mountains, greenbelt, or golf courses.

- In many cities, you will find that homes located within walking distance of recreational opportunities such as entertainment, or movie theaters, parks, and golf courses are more expensive than properties located further away.

- Neighborhoods that have stood the test of time and are more likely to have stable home values in the community.

Locations with lower home values

have better supply and lower demand for homes. More people want to measure in Honolulu than in Decatur. Home values also vary by neighborhood within a given area. What factors reduce home values?

Commercial buildings on the verge of residential property can reduce land values. Part of the reasoning for this is that homeowners cannot control the noise, traffic, and other activities that accompany commercial development. Another factor is that commercial property is considered separate from residential. Like economic buildings, there is an impression on home values. Retail development may increase home values after construction ends, but during construction, the home value may fall.

Rail tracks, overpasses, airports, and busy intersections can cause more noise in homes. This will also reduce property values.

High crime rates in neighborhoods typically lower property values.

A dangerous situation in a neighborhood can lower property values. Although housing developments are initially located far away from any hazardous conditions, problems can develop over time. Toxic emissions from industrial plants affect air quality and lower domestic prices. Sinkholes have been visible in Florida for many years, declining property values in vulnerable areas.

When circumstances change, even when you find a range at the desired location that looks like fair value, it never hurts to think of additional factors that will affect the property within the future. Ask about any new or planned construction nearby or vacant land that will be developed within the future.

Sometimes, in new home development, zoning, and building plans change. An example could also be a buyer buying a house because the ground broke during new construction on an empty floor behind the house. Instead of having planned single-family homes, the developer builds apartment buildings. Apartment buildings change the entire landscape, and hence the formerly attractive views of the homeowner are now interrupted. This may be the reason for the lower selling price in the future.

The centrality where you choose to measure within a city or town will undoubtedly affect your home buying ratio. Land can be a finite commodity, so cities like San Francisco that are highly developed and do not have tons of room for additional development possess higher prices than cities that have an excessive amount of room to expand. Many of the households in these communities are uninhabited, and some areas have become dislocated. In most cases, this increase is the result of a boost, consistent with the Bureau of U.S. Census data on urban areas. When the sprawling city experiences a population exodus, it is the outlying areas that suffer the most significant decline in property value.

The neighborhood that appeals to you is mostly a matter of personal choice. However, a very great neighborhood would have some significant factors: access, presence, and amenities. Your community can set many dimensions for building your home.

In terms of accessibility, you should look for an area located near the major thoroughfares of your city, with a point of entry. Working and going can be a big part of many people's day, so a house with quick access to roads and public transport is going to be more desirable than one that is tucked away and can only be reached by one route.

Neighborhood presence is additionally essential. Large trees, landscaping and surrounding green or community spaces are desirable. You will also support the neighborhood's recognition of how long areas of homes will remain on the market. If a turnover occurs quickly, you are not the only person who thinks that this is often a desirable place to measure.

A great neighborhood should also include essential facilities such as grocery stores, shops, and restaurants. Most people repeatedly desire convenient places — if you must travel an excellent distance to insist on anything, it is likely to make your home less attractive.

Schools are another important feature — even if you do not have children, if you want to sell your range over the long term, many buyers are permanent seekers. There are essential factors to think about, both the standard of local schools and therefore the distance from home.

Lastly, do not forget security. An area that features low rates and is an inviting and safe place to be outside and commune with neighbors is the kind of place most people want to measure.

Development

It is not only the facilities that matter, but also the future. Plans for schools, hospitals, public transport, and other public infrastructure can dramatically improve property values within the region. Professional development can also enhance property values. When you are purchasing a home, try to determine if a new public, commercial, or residential development is planned, and consider how these additions may affect the desirability of the areas involved.

The proximity of a property to a fire station, hospital, school, or civic center can reduce its value due to traffic and noise.

Lot location

You also must keep in mind where exactly the house is located. During this example, there are some items that you should limit your mind to as well as to conduct your search.

If the house you want to shop for is on a busy street or near the highway, you will probably catch on at a lower cost, but it will also be harder to sell later. An equivalent house may be right for homes that stand on or behind a commercial property or like a grocery or gasoline station, or homes on streets that are primarily used for parking traffic and parked cars near churches or community centers. Receive an unusual amount.

Alternatively, a house with an excellent view or near a body of water is probably going to be more valuable, both now and when it comes time to sell it.

The house itself tends to surprise people that house hunting is not an aspect. For example, you have limited your choice to 2 homes that stand shoulder to shoulder during a great neighborhood. Repairs and updates are needed, but a much larger feature. In contrast, the tiptop is shaped but sits on the tanker at half the upper dimension. The cost of 2 houses is the same. Which one chooses? In most cases, homes requiring repairs are a better investment.

Reason: Your house is a depreciation asset. The lot, on the opposite hand, will maintain its value (or appreciation of probability) relative to the house. If you bulldoze both homes, the larger lot will sell for more; therefore, if you choose a much larger, better shape or better located above a good place. A less attractive home can always be updated, added, or completely replaced, but not much can be changed.

CHAPTER 4
Build your team

Most agents dream of the day they can make their first hire.

But those who have done it know that often it is crucial fun.

(And by 'fun' we mean, not only large incomes but all the high-level challenges and leadership headaches that accompany it.) Get your home so that your revenue initiatives can help your revenue goals while building a dedicated property team. To complete work backward to ensure what percentage of leads and team members will be needed to satisfy you. As a team leader, your actual role is that of the Chief Lead Generator, so confirm that your systems are in a battle of size and ready to handle growth within the number of leads that come in handy.

To line up the real estate system:

· *Team Land Business Plan & Goals*

· *Vision, Purpose, & Brand*

· *Marketing & Advertising*

· *Database & Referral System*

· *Listing & Farming System*

· *Buyer, Escrow, & Transaction Management System*

· *Lead generation and follow-up system*

· *Internet and Social Media Marketing*

· *Financial, productivity, profitability reports, and forecasts that give whom rent received.*

First, despite the mountains of recommendations against it, many agents still start adding the buyer's agents before they require their core business systems in situ.

But buyer's agents should be rainmakers, not admin whiskeys. Your land system must run like a Swiss watch so that when your high-octane agents come on board, they will just connect and keep going - without getting a clunky workflow.

If you have not found the time to urge your home, you will take two critical steps to hire your administrator first.

Agents who close 30 consecutive deals for a year should have no problem helping a full-time administrator. But if you are drowning in paperwork and are confident that you will have a transaction soon, there are also some flexible (and inexpensive) remote options, including Myotubes and Virtual Assistant Staffing.

Buyer Agent

Now that you have got the paperwork off your plate and the ability to travel across your system, you can unload many of these results from an ace buyer specialist.

The buyer agent's top priority is to ensure that no lead slips through the crack. You want to supply them with a ready-made rock-solid lead farming strategy, and they should be able to follow inventory maintenance and follow-ups.

Your buyer agent must be ready to handle a maximum of 4 transactions per month. When this is the case, when you can cross that number (do a touch dance), prepare to cause your second agent or ISA.

Inside the sales agent,

Once you have your dedicated buyer agent, you are generous to get out there and generate a lot more listings. Things are getting increasingly busy, all the way around. Now, your team is hugely tempted to focus solely on new leads and short-term deals.

Now is the right time to enter your first ISA. An excellent ISA can only double its GCI, which tries to pick up agents they do not want to try, namely: making phone calls.

Mitch Roebuck (aka The Grandfather of Lead Conversion) is the founding father and former broker-owner of InsularAgents.com, at Tropical Realty Beachside in Melbourne, FL. Mitch has used

ISAs to realize $ 127 million in annual transaction volume and to increase conversion rates by 450%.

But be forewarned: faster, frequent followings will lead to more leads and more contracts. You, your system, and your agents were able to hit bottom running.

Listing the agent is as the owner of the business, to ensure that you always get the proper number of listings.

You need to keep your team busy throughout the year, while you have proved that the volume of transactions increases steadily from month to month.

When you reach the height for the number of lists, you will manage yourself (e.g., if you are building a vendor from the hotel business center on your family's "holiday"), then it will help in time. It is time to rent—either a listing agent/expert or transaction coordinator.

You may prefer to hire a VA as your transaction coordinator. Tools like Brown and Brown or Admin You sometimes have a fee range of $ 300- $ 700 per transaction and are an efficient, inexpensive option for renting in-house.

Other roles

Every time you hit a replacement revenue target, it is time to gauge your team and consider bringing in more help.

There are many ways for you to develop your team, including marketing directors, assistants, and even personal assistants. How you choose, your team will depend entirely on your goals for your life and your business.

Do Your Math is underestimated by many agent teams. A primary reason is that they pay other agents at a full rate rather than at the expense of their post-partition.

If you are putting in the time and energy required to build a terrific land team, then you confirm getting the math right from the beginning. The last item you want seems to be at some point, and you feel like you own a business that makes $10 an hour.

Do not forget small things.

One of the biggest common mistakes you start making is ignoring the small things that led to your growth in the first place.

Joe Arsenio, director and agent of residential sales at Open Listing, was facing a drastic increase in volume after his team decided to grow.

"When I arrived at 20 Escrows and remained between 20-30 Scours for a few weeks at least, I knew that the time had come to produce more team members. My fellow agents were also within the same boat. More than all of us were accepting that we were closing (escrow is usually 30 days and thus the closing month is over), and yet the leads continued to flow at an increasing rate. We would love to hire more agents to ensure that we do not stumble upon our top-notch service".

Joe and his team have hired more showing agents, internal customer service representatives, and transaction coordinators to ensure that they are prepared to maintain excellent service all the way.

According to Joe, the # 1 most important "little thing" is instant communication. Whether it is a response to a primary time check, or managing the escrow process, Joe and his teams aim to respond to all or any inquiries within 1 hour, if not immediately - even if it is just to accept the difficulty. And address to be addressed to the customer. Being organized and responsive means the world to a buyer.

"Above and beyond answering an issue. Be proactive with your responses so that your customer does not need to locate the appropriate inquiry to ask. More information and knowledge will make your customer feel comfortable that you have got their back," he advises.

Whoever advises agents and their teams to leave the jargon, clients do not understand the critical property process, and that is why they have hired you. He encourages his teams to talk to customers and prospects as if they could speak to a lover. "Defer to the point of sales and change humanity." The goal is to make the customer feel comfortable and happy at the top of the transaction.

Hire Rights

" I had systems in situ to mold the necessary skill sets and market knowledge, but personalities are some things you just can't teach." - Jake Tasha sky, Center Coast Realty Wells While

When you are moving at 100 mph from appointment to appointment, it is often unbelievable to rent the initial set of hands. But beware, lousy work costs time and money.

When Chicago brokers, Jake Tasha sky, started hiring his first Rainmaker, he knew culture and personality would be a priority. He wanted it to represent his brand and emulate the experience of his customers.

And he made sure he had a solid plan for onboarding. Jake brought his first agent, Sarah Troy, during and she shadowed him one day for the primary few months on the job. By the time the busy season rolled around, she was ready to cover and show off her rental business fully.

Whatever you want to understand team dynamics,

Most agents agree that excellent team dynamics are essential, but not everyone goes the extra mile to work appropriately with how their team ticks.

Here is a fast part of the influential personality inventory tool to help you choose which is right for you.

The disc is far from a four-transit personality list and a widely used team-building tool within the land industry (and with over 1 million people using it per year, it will be the most popular term). The greatest strength of Disc is its simplicity.

Each team member is asked to rate their instinct towards each of the latter's characteristics:

- dominance - direct, strong-willed and forceful

- influence - sociable, talkative and lively

- stability - gentle, sociable and soft-hearted

- conscience. -, personal, analytical and logical

Based on their Disc profile, team members and leaders determine the simplest thanks to the interaction with each other.

For example, a high D is going to be most motivating when you demonstrate your passion for certain goals..

While someone with a high C wants naughty kitty details on how and why this goal was created, of course, someone can be high on both D and C, and for those team members, you want to appeal to both their enthusiasm and their desire for the details of desire.

The Myers-Briggs

Myers-Briggs Type Indicator (MBTI) is widely used as a bus and is revered at DESC. The biggest difference is that Disc assesses how people behave externally, while the MBTI is more competent towards the interior, such as how people think, feel, and make decisions.

The MBTI is longer than the Disc, which has 16 four-letter personality types:

Extraversion (E) / Introversion (I) - Extraverted types of people learn best by interacting with others. Introverted types prefer quiet reflection and privacy.

Sensing (S) / Intuition (I) - Sensing types enjoy a learning environment where situations are presented in a detailed, sequential manner. Spontaneous types prefer learning environments where a strain is placed on meanings and associations.

Thinking (T) / Feeling (F) - Thinking types aspire to objective truth and logical principles and are naturals at deduction. The feeling classes emphasize issues and reasons that would be personal when considering other people's motives.

Judging (J) / Perceiving (P) - The judging types will thrive when information is organized and structured, and they are motivated to complete assignments to realize closure. Perceiving types will flourish during a flexible learning environment, during which new and exciting ideas inspire them.

Category 1 - Producers and Separable. All you must do is give these agents a general direction; they are highly motivated and can take on any task and get on with it.

Category 2 - Productive and Unbearable. These people are often extraordinarily successful, but you have to follow them; they do not want to tell you what to try.

Category 3 - Unproductive and Coachable. These agents are mating, but they are trapped during a rut. They have small, manageable activities and action steps (huge goals and no consequences) to urge them to return within the game.

Category 4 - Unproductive and Unnatural- There are approximately 600,000 types of agents within the land industry. These people will not be your rock stars, but they will do OK during brokerage with low fees and low expectations.

Use your intuition

In the 20 years game, Kyle knows one or two things about hiring a team. The Dublin, Ohio Realtor uses "independently integrated" slogans to remind team members of the importance of being self-motivated, and looking at the big picture, a trait he is had to live with in trials.

But he has also made some mistakes within the past, and now Kyle works slowly.

First, his staff conducts an initial phone screening.

Next is an interview, including some Myers-Briggs tests that focus on the most, to remove bad candidates, such as to find great ones.

In the end, Kyle gets the candidate. "Out of the box 'I will like them, which is marketing and sales, the more I follow my stomach. However, on more procedural or compliance related jobs, such as closing coordinators or processors, the more I make decisions." Questionnaires and personality tests allow, "Kyle explains.

Ultimately, no matter the situation, Kyle always supported the final call in the gut. Laughs.

Why

According to Kent Clothier, land training and wholesaler boss, your team is there to push your business forward and help your customers while entrepreneurs put pressure on you. Micromanage defeats the purpose of being

"In my experience, the current key is great to live in rent to the appropriate people and healthy system. However, none of it matters that your team does not collide with purpose-driven people. They clearly understand why they are the neighborhood of your organization and feel compelled to try to make you and your organization do more."

Once you recognize the personality and productivity styles of your employees, you get to know tons about what motivates them. Align your drivers with the overall mission of the business, and you will get them to keep you up and running every day.

CHAPTER 5
Line Up Financing

A LOC is an appointment between a financial institution - usually a bank - and a customer who establishes the maximum amount of loan that the customer can borrow. Borrowers can use the funds from the road of credit at any time, as long as they do not exceed the maximum amount (or credit limit) set within the agreement and meet other requirements such as making minimum payments on time. It will be offered as a convenience.

Understanding the Line of Credit

All LOCs have a set amount of cash that is borrowed, paid back, and re-borrowed as needed. The lender determines the amount of interest, size of the payment, and other rules. Some lines of credit allow you to write a check (draft), while others include a type of credit or open-ended credit. As noted above, a LOC is often secured (by collateral) or unsecured, unsecured LOCs are usually subject to a higher interest rate.

A line of credit has inherent flexibility, which is its main advantage. Borrowers can request a specific amount, but they are not required to use it. Instead, they will record their spending on the LOC for their needs and pay interest only on their credit amount, not the entire credit line. Additionally, borrowers can adjust their repayment amount as needed, supporting their budget or income. For example, they will pay the whole outstanding balance directly or pay only the minimum monthly.

Unsecured vs. Secured LOC

Most lines of credit are unsecured loans. This suggests that the borrower does not promise any collateral to return the LOC. A notable exception may be the domestic equity line of credit (HELOC), which is secured by equity within the borrower's home. From a lender's point of view, secured lines of credit are attractive because of how they repurchase advanced funds in the event of non-payment.

For individuals or business owners, secured lines of credit are attractive because they typically have a better maximum credit limit and a significantly lower interest rate than unsecured lines of credit.

Unsecured lines of credit return with higher interest rates than secured LOCs. They are also harder to get and sometimes require a better credit score or credit rating. Borrowers plan to increase the risk that they limit by charging the amount borrowed and higher interest rates. Therefore, the APR on credit cards is high. Credit cards are technically unsecured credit lines, representing the parameters of how much you will charge on the menu, along with the credit limit. But after opening a cardboard account, you are not pledging any property. If you start paying, there is nothing the MasterCard Issuer can seize in compensation.

A reversionary line of credit offered by a bank or financial organization to a private or business organization may be a source of debt that will be canceled at the discretion of the lender or under specific circumstances. A bank or financial organization can cancel a line of credit if the customer's financial circumstances deteriorate, or if market conditions become so unfavorable on warrant revocation, such as after the 2008 global debt crisis. A reversible line of credit is often unsecured or secured, with an interest rate generally better than before.

Credit vs. Non-Revolving Lines of Credit

A line is generally regarded as a revolving account, also known as a revolving credit account. This arrangement allows borrowers to spend cash, repay it, and spend it again during an almost never-ending, revolving cycle. Stories revolving credit and credit card lines differ from installment loans such as mortgages, car loans, and signature loans.

With installment loans, also known as closed-end credit accounts, consumers pay off an amount of the loan and repay it in equal monthly installments until the loan is repaid. Once the installment credit has been paid, consumers cannot spend the money again until they apply for a replacement loan.

Non-revolving lines of credit have a facility equivalent to open-ended credit (or revolving line of credit). A credit limit is established, money is often used for purposes of dissemination, interest is usually charged, and payments can be made at any time. One major exception is: The pool of debt receivable does not refill after payment is received. Once you pay off the road of credit in full, the account is closed and cannot be used again.

As an example, individual lines of credit are sometimes offered by banks as a type of overdraft protection scheme. A banking customer can check the overdraft scheme linked to his bank account. If the customer exceeds the available quantity in the checking, the overdraft prevents them from bouncing the check or denying the sale. Like all lines of credit, an overdraft must be paid back, including interest.

Examples of lines of credit

They are available in a proliferation of LOC forms, each of which falls under the safe or unsafe category. In addition, each type of LOC has its characteristics.

Personal Line of Credit

This provides access to unsecured funds that will be borrowed, repaid, and re-borrowed. Opening a private line of credit requires a credit history without default, a credit score of 680 or more and a reliable income. It is helping savings as collateral in a stock or CD type, although collateral is not required for private LOCs. Personal LOCs are used for emergencies, weddings, and other events, overdraft protection, travel and recreation, and to help smooth bumps for people with irregular incomes.

Home Equity Line of Credit (HELOC)

HELOCs are the most common type of secured LOC. A HELOC is secured by the market value of the minus balance of the house, which becomes the consideration for determining the dimensions of the street of credit. Typically, the credit limit is enough for 75% or 80% of the market value of the home, minus the outstanding balance on the mortgage.

HELOCs often occur with a draw period (typically ten years), during which the borrower can access the available funds, repay them, and borrow again. After the draw period, the balance is owed, or a loan is extended to pay off the balance over time. MOOCs typically have closing costs, including the value of the valuation on the asset used as collateral. After the passage of the Tax Cuts and Jobs Act of 2017, interest paid on HOOCs is only deducted if the funds are accustomed to buy, build or improve the property that is collateral for the chopper.

This type is often secured or unsecured but never used. With a requirement LOC, the lender can call the amount borrowed at any time. Paybacks (unless called loans) are often interest-only or interest plus principal, which are counted on the terms of the LOC the borrower can spend up to the credit limit at any time.

Securities-backed line of credit (SBLOC)

This is a special secured-demand LOC, during which the borrower's securities provide collateral. Typically, an SBLOC allows an investor to borrow anywhere from 50% to 95% of the value of the asset in their account. SBLOCs are non-objective loans, which means that the borrower cannot use cash or purchase trade securities. Almost any other type of expenditure is allowed.

The SBLOC requires the borrower to make monthly, interest-only payments until the loan is repaid in full or demands a brokerage or bank payment, which can occur if the value of the investor's portfolio is the road of credit falls below the limit.

A business line of credit businesses

Use these to borrow on an as-needed basis rather than removing a hard and fast loan. The LOC expanding financial organization evaluates the market value, profitability, and risk taken by the business and extends a line of credit supporting that analysis. The LOC can also be unsecured or secured; it counts on the dimensions of the route of credit requested and hence the evaluation result. Like most LOCs, the rate of interest is variable.

Limitations of lines of credit

The main advantage of a line is the ability to borrow only the required amount and avoid paying interest on external debt. Borrowers should remember potential problems when removing a line of credit.

Unsecured LOCs have higher interest rates and loan requirements than the collateral rate.

Interest rates (APRs) for lines of credit are almost always variable and vary widely from one lender to another.

Lines of credit do not provide the same regulatory protection as credit cards. Penalties are often severe for late-payments and exceeding the LOC limit.

An open line of credit may invite over speeding, resulting in an inability to pay.

Misuse of a line of credit can damage a borrower's credit score.

As an early investor, understanding how to finance a deal is as important as finding someone. The lack of land financing remains a hindrance to the bulk of the latest investors in today's market, simply because they are not conscious of the various financing avenues. Whether or not you have access to capital, there are always ways to accumulate capital.

Financing real estate may be generally habitual for an investor to describe an investor's method of acquiring funds for an imminent transaction. As its name suggests, this method requires investors to secure capital from an external source so that a property can be purchased and renovated. Unlike conventional financing, however, land financing is met with conditions and underwriting, not for the smallest amount that must be fully understood before coming into a contract.

One of the most important misconceptions of land investment is that you must start soliciting for tons, which is simply not true. However, many professionals do not understand that the various land financing options available to fund every investment are flawed. Because the strategy during which a selected deal is financed can affect its outcome, it is crucial to understand the financing aspect.

As an investor, there are some alternative ways to travel about financing land investments. Everyone will have their own set of pros and cons, and your financing approach will depend on the property and, therefore, the situation. For early investors, it is essential to remember that not all land investment financing options are created equal. What works for someone else may not be necessary for you, but the trick is knowing which land financing option will compliment your business strategy. By taking the time to research various land financing options, new investors are bound to realize how often the investment is accessible. Expanding the toolkit of one of the land investment financing options is simply a matter of getting intimate about whether the strategies exist, as well as the appropriate ways to leverage them. Assume that every single investor has faced a funding constraint at some point in their career; While unsure, there is nothing wrong with tapping into your investor network and inviting advice.

Real estate financial options

investors with a deal have already completed one of the most critical stages in house flipping. However, finding a viable deal is only one piece of the puzzle. Once you have discovered an honest property, you want to be ready for the next transaction.

Enough to send new investors into a fit of frenzy in a dedicated property deal, or to force them to shut down their dreams and withdraw at their nine-to-five jobs. However, if an investor works diligently, the possibility of a lack of funds is irrational.

If you find an excellent deal on the table, there is no limit to including ways to fund it. An excellent example would be taking advantage of a self-directed IRA, which may require some careful consideration beforehand. However, this indicates that there are several available options for financing land investment. In considering how to support an investment property for investors, I will explain your several land financings options:

Cash Financing: For investors who have access to large amounts of capital, either personally or through their network, there is access, and there is a need to get the qualities free and clear.

Hard Money Lenders: For those investors who have a low-to-perfect credit or financial history and need short-term loans.

Private Money Lenders: Investors who are well connected can often tap into the capital from personal connections, borrowing money at a specified interest rate and payback period.

Self-directed IRA Accounts: Individuals who have chosen to save through self-directed IRAs can choose to tap into their account how to use the capital.

Seller Financing: Buyers and sellers can sometimes strike an interdependent agreement, allowing investors and sellers to avoid traveling through the individual lender entirely.

Cash Financing: As an investor, cash can be a great tool you want. With more offers accepted, cash financing enables investors to save much interest, increase their income, and get immediate equity in their investments. It also has the power to save many investors on the acquisition amount.

In the 2016 half-moon, all cash for single-family homes conformed to homebuyers and reattract, on average, 23 percent less per square foot than all homebuyers nationwide.

Also, it is essential to remember that there will be times when it makes sense to pay cash for a property and other times when other financing options should be considered. If you have got your capital, however, you should always think about using it in the best scenarios.

Hard Money Lenders

Financed by private businesses and individuals, hard money lenders offer short-term, high-rate loans to land investors. This financing option, which does not conform to bank standards of loan worthiness, is typically employed by reinsurers looking to renovate a property.

Hard money financing is usually determined by the value of the investment property by analyzing the "after repair value" (ARV) by lenders to find out the dimensions of the loan.

Generally, hard money lenders will not fund the entire deal but will receive a percentage of the acquisition price or post-repair value, which can range from 50 to 70 percent.

Also, hard money lenders charge a separate fee from interest on the loan. These fees are usually distributed in points (three to five), representing additional percentage fees that support the loan amount. Generally, hard money lenders charge a much higher interest rate - sometimes double the amount of a standard mortgage, plus fees. In the end, all hard money lenders will have different requirements, and land investors must be fully conscious of what they are doing in themselves.

Private Money Lenders

They are integral to the expansion of each new investor. They need the means and intention to take a position in your business, and they are also as curious about working with you as you are with them.

Generally, private money lenders provide investors with cash to obtain property in exchange for the chosen interest rate. These conditions will typically be established upfront and with a specified payback period - anywhere from six months to a year. These loans are regular when investors believe they will increase the value of a specific asset in a short period, usually through renewal. It is also essential to know that, as hard money, private money should only be used when you have a clearly defined exit strategy.

Self-Directed IRA Account

A self-directed IRA (Individual Retirement Account) is, at its primary level, a bank account that allows for compounded, tax-free growth over time. Self-directed IRAs are unique from other types of savings accounts, like the 401K, as owners can control a good array of investment options, including land.

Owners of self-directed IRA accounts have a unique advantage of having the ability to acquire, rehab, and sell property, despite having the ability to collect taxes. However, it is essential to note that owners under the age of 60 are generally subject to penalties for quickly withdrawing money.

Vendor financing

There are some scenarios when both an investor and a seller can strike a mutually beneficial seller financing deal. In seller financing, the customer of the property will pay the seller of the property, instead of browsing the bank. This will help a motivated seller sell the property more quickly, and so investors can avoid leaping over traditional mortgage loan barriers such as financial and credit score minimums.

Together, customers and vendors can often enjoy a faster transaction process, also avoiding many costs and costs related to the closing process. Also, the owner has the option to sell the note if they do not wish to manage their financing.

Best Loans for Land Investment

When examining the vast umbrella of various land financing options, one should also consider the loans offered by the government, traditional lenders, as ways to leverage personal equity. Read on to find one of the most popular loan options used creatively by investors, including Land Investment Loans on Bad Debt.

203K Loans: A particular type of loan backed by the Federal Housing Administration, 203K Loans for Acquisition.

Home Equity Loan: Homeowners who have built up equity within their property are ready to remove a loan like a line of credit, allowing them to expand their portfolio using their equity as collateral.

FHA Loan: Consumers with less-than-perfect debt, or who do not have access to deposit capital, can gain ownership of the home by removing a mortgage backed by the Federal Housing Administration to complete a deposit capital.

Traditional Mortgage Loans: Traditional home loans financed by banks are still one of the favorite ways of funding of land deals.

Conforming Loan: As its name suggests, a conforming loan can be a mortgage that is established by or enough for the conforming loan limit set by the FHFA. Maybe even more importantly, conforming loans follow the Federal Home Loan Mortgage Corporation and the Federal National Mortgage Association.

Portfolio Loans: Portfolio loans are serviced by the initial lenders who previously issued funds. However, instead of selling the loan to the secondary market, the service provider will keep the loan in its portfolio.

VA Loan: A VA loan can be a mortgage guaranteed by the US Department of Affairs.

203K Loans

203K loans are a particular type of loan supported by the Federal Housing Administration and are mainly for those who decide to rehabilitate old or damaged properties. The loan also includes the value of the acquisition of the property, as well as the estimated cost to renew. 203K rehab loans are attractive to some due to a low deposit requirement of 3.5 percent and allow for the financing of cosmetic or significant repairs when necessary. Additionally, the borrower can include the value of six months of mortgage payment within the loan.

This policy is intended to assist homeowners in making mortgage payments during periods that they cannot sleep in the property during their rehabilitation phase. However, investors should remember some possible downgrades for current particular loans. First, 203K borrowers are required to hire a licensed contractor and construction consultant, meaning DIY projects are not permitted. Additionally, fix and flip investment properties are not eligible. They will be ready for an owner-occupied approach by purchasing a property with one to four units.

Home Equity Loan

When an investor has built equity within the type of their residence, they require a loan against that equity. A home equity loan, formally known as the Home Equity Line of Credit (HELOC), allows homeowners to leverage their home equity as collateral so that a loan is needed. Common uses for home equity loans include home repair, education, or debt resolution.

A significant advantage of a home equity loan is that a low prime rate generally backs the coffee shop. Additionally, lenders enjoy the feasibility of using the loan to decide how they might like it, as well as managing their repayment structure. This flexibility creates an opportunity for homeowners to expand their portfolio on their terms.

FHA loan

FHA loan is one of several home equity credit options offered by the federal. The Federal Housing Administration (FHA) established a loan to help broad-based access to homework for consumers with a less-than-perfect credit profile, even for those who must save lots for external deposits. They are not financial instruments. When homebuyer shops a replacement for real estate loan options, they will look for lenders who offer real estate loan products that are supported by the FHA. These loans offer deposits as low as 3.5 percent, while still allowing for an interest rate.

However, it should be noted that putting 20 percent down on a domestic equity credit will eliminate a required private mortgage insurance payment. Additionally, the FHA loan only permits owner-authorized properties but leaves the acquisition of an asset with substantially one unit. According to The Lenders Network, the current loan limit for a single unit asset is between $ 294,515 to $ 679,650, which calculates whether the market can be a low-cost or high-cost sector.

Traditional Real Estate Loan

One of the more popular financing methods in land is through traditional lenders, which include conventional and FHA loans. Many investors are pursuing standard lender financing options in today's market as interest rates are at historic lows.

However, traditional lenders follow strict guidelines with many demands that do not require other financing options. Obstacles with conventional loans, like a standard real estate loan, include a substantial deposit (from 15 to 25 percent), an adequate credit score (a minimum of 680), and income documentation. Additionally, the cash used should be called "SONS-and CZ" for a minimum of 60 days, which may not currently occur. In many cases, this can limit many investors.

Construction loans correspond to loans, as shown in their name, following the Federal National Mortgage Association and the Federal Home Loan standardized rules laid down by the Mortgage Corporation. More specifically, however, a portion of these loans are "tailored," indicating the amount borrowed. Conforming loans are set by the Federal Housing Finance Agency but should have a conforming lending limit. The 2019 end for confirmed loans is approximately $ 484,350, or $ 31,250, the corresponding loan limit for the previous year. However, it is worth noting that the simulation-lending end is not universal in every market. In high-value areas such as Ni or San Diego, the range is higher.

Outside of the loan dimensions, analogous loans are also characterized by the following:

- Debt-to-value ratio

- Debt-to-income ratio

- Credit score and history

- Documentation requirements

Portfolio Debt

Portfolios are not financed by the loan originator, but instead a secondary market. Being sold in - as most traditional lenders do - lenders create loans for their portfolios, Kegan. As a result, borrowers will not need to establish a relationship with another lender and, instead, can maintain the context of their current lender. In other words, it would be straightforward to take care of an open line of communication.

VA Loan

VA Loan serve Veterans, Service Members, and their Spouse. VA loans are issued by qualified lenders and are guaranteed by the US Department of Affairs (VA). Specifically, the VA will guarantee a maximum of 25 percent of the home equity credit amount of up to $ 113,275, which limits the maximum loan amount to $ 453,100. According to VAloans.com, meanwhile, "the fair value of the property or the price of the acquisition, whichever is a small amount, as well as money charges, can be borrowed."

Using lender financing can be an excellent option for beginner investors, but it is essential to bend my thumbs and get ready. Confirm that you understand the method and what is required to request approval.

CHAPTER 6
Plan to find a deal

Treat Investments as Businesses

Land investors must set their land activities as a business and set and achieve short- and long-term goals. A business plan allows land investors to identify not only objectives but also determine a viable course of action that results in their realization. A business plan also allows investors to see the bigger picture, which helps to specialize in goals rather than any minor setbacks. Land investment is often complex and demanding, and a sound plan can keep investors organized and on task.

Know Your Markets

Influential land investors gain in-depth knowledge of their selected market (s). The more an investor understands a specific need, the more qualified he or she is to make sound business decisions. Considering the current trends, including any changes in consumer spending habits, mortgage rates, and, therefore, the percentage from which to call a couple, savvy investors are required in current circumstances, and long-term planning. Being interactive in specific markets allows investors to anticipate when trends are changing, creating potentially beneficial opportunities.

Maintain High Ethical Standards

Realtors are bound by a code of ethics and industry standards, while land agents are held to the principles and standards of the Land Commission of every state. On the other hand, if they do not belong to membership-based organizations, and if they operate within the boundaries of the law, land investors generally do not need to take care of ethics-based practices. While it may be easy for them to benefit from dishonesty, most successful land investors maintain high ethical standards. Since land investment involves actively working with people, an investor's reputation is probably going to be far-reaching. The consequences of a lack of morality for an investor are often harmful, especially at the end of the day. Influential land investors realize that it is best to conduct the business impartially, rather than what they will avoid.

Develop a focus or niche

Because there are many ways to take a position in the ground, investors must develop attention to realize the depth of data needed to become successful. It involves learning everything, certain kinds of investment - be it wholesale sales or commercial land - and building confidence in it. Taking time to understand this level is integral to the long-term success of the investor. Once a specific market is mastered, the investor can progress into additional areas. Savvy investors know that it is better to try to do five things well than to do bad things.

Get good at customer service

Referral generates a large part of a dedicated property investor's business, so it is vital that investors treat others with respect. This includes business partners, associates, customers, tenants, and anyone with whom the investor accounts. Influential land investors are good at customer service, especially in listening to detail, responding to complaints and concerns, and representing their business positively and professionally.

Be Educated

As with any business, it is imperative to keep up with the laws, regulations, terminology, and trends that make up the business idea of a critical property investor. Work is required to maintain the current, but it is often seen as an investment in the way forward for the business.

If laws are ignored or broken, successful land investors take time and make it difficult to stay educated due to any regulatory changes or adapting to economic trends.

Understand the risks that choosing to take a position within the stock or futures market has given numerous warnings about the risks inherent in investing. Many agencies, such as the Commodity Futures Trading Commission, require disclaimers to warn potential market participants about the possibility of a loss of capital. While most of this is legal, it is clear to people that investing in the stock or futures market is risky; This means that a person can have several tons of cash. Greenhorn land investors, however, are only likely to be bombarded with advertisements claiming the other - that it is easy to make money in the land. Prudent land investors understand business-related risks -

not only in the context of land deals but also legal implications - and adjust their businesses to scale back any risk.

Work with a reputable accountant covers a large portion of the annual expenses of a dedicated property investor in taxes. Current tax laws are not easy to understand and take too much time away from the business.. Sharp land investors retain the services of a professional, reputable accountant to handle business books. Accountant-related values are often salvable, which may be negligible compared to savings experts.

Once they get the help they need, real estate investing is complex and requires excellent experience to negotiate profitably within the business. Learning the business and, therefore, the legal process is challenging anyone to try to travel it alone. Influential land investors often give a portion of their success to others - whether a custodian, lawyer, accountant, or supportive friend. Instead of spending time and money solving a difficult problem on their own, successful investors realize that it is worth the extra cost to seek help when needed and embrace other people's expertise.

Build a Network. A network can provide significant support and provide opportunities for new and experienced land investors alike to build a brand. This group of associates is often made up of a well-chosen patron, business partners, customers, or a non-profit organization that has an interest in the land. A network allows investors to challenge and support each other and can significantly assist in advancing one's career through shared knowledge and new opportunities.

Because much of land investment relies on experience-based education, savvy land investors understand the importance of building a network, rather than bookish knowledge.

A growing number of the latest and experienced land investors are taking advantage of the convenience of online marketplaces to search for rental property. There are two main reasons for this:

Reason # 1: Much of the "heavy lifting" of detecting and analyzing deals is already done. You only must choose from the options that are the simplest match for your land investment strategy.

Reason # 2: Out-of-market investment is straightforward. Diversifying the portfolio of rental properties geographically helps minimize risk and maximize reward by seizing opportunities that often cannot be found in your backyard.

Global land marketplaces allow global capital markets such as real capital markets and GREM investors to buy and sell property worldwide. Initially, investing may seem like a beautiful option.

However, the complexities of international law, fluctuations in currency exchange rates, and therefore the threat of ongoing trade wars create potential problems for international land investors that are not found here within the US,

While crowdfunding is not technically a market, crowdfunding sites pool land investors. His money with other investors to shop for commercial property, multi-family, and single-family homes, all of which are listed online.

While crowdfunding can be a great way to diversify investment capital, one of the most significant drawbacks is that your options are limited. Instead of a direct share of the substantial asset, you receive a small portion of the entity that owns the critical support. There are some benefits of partial ownership of land, but investors should have freedom of choice.

Single-Family Rental (SFR)

A recent article by the National Land Investor states that the single-family rental (SFR) sector still proliferates, with many land markets showing the growth of three to five or more.

CNBC noted how the build-to-rent housing market is exploding as investors participate in it, while Forbes writes that housing stock is not keeping up with demand. Situations such as these can provide an excellent potential for investors who own income assets.

There is a proliferation of operators of online marketplaces for single-family land investors. Small sector-specific players specialize in niche markets only, while sizeable national investment platforms such as Rootstock literally must deal with multiple households on any given day.

Suggestions for locating deals on MLS

Good land deals can also be found on MLS; You only watch to know. The good thing about many listing services is that this land is full of all kinds of useful information for investors.

Foreclose

Lenders or landlords who do not continue with their mortgage obligations. The foreclosure process varies from state to state, but there is a "window of opportunity" for investors to shop from home before the owner tampers with the property. Many homeowners facing foreclosure inspire sellers to avoid the stigma of losing their home to the bank and bad credit.

REO: Once the foreclosure process is over, the property owned by the land is with the bank. Banks are not within the business of owning land, and an REO asset represents a non-performing loan to the bank. Repeated banks urge the property of their books to sell to an investor for less.

Auctions Property: Homes are auctioned by banks, as furnished for property or unpaid property taxes by the county. Auctions are often a source of excellent deals for investors, but they also carry a high degree of risk because sales are "as-is" and must be purchased in cash.

Every successful land investor undertakes some marketing campaign at any given time. The key to finding more land deals is to diversify your marketing efforts. By doing this, investors can further expand their overall reach before the competition.

The biggest challenge when it involves marketing is knowing which option is best for you. Many investors consider spam and bandit signals helpful, while others prefer social media and networking. But finding the appropriate combination of techniques for your market is the simplest thanks to generating consistent, reliable leads. Read through our guide below and find out how to get good land deals today.

To seek the simplest land deal, you want to travel the extra mile and not come to the market with your competition methods. It suggests honoring those who work in your area (and what does not) to spot the simplest leads. An honest place to start is by researching various marketing strategies and testing them in your area. Through careful planning and implementation, you will find options that are both cost-effective and efficient.

The list below reveals several marketing ideas that will assist you in generating reliable land deals:

Direct Mail

Facebook

Other Land Professional

Driving for Dollars

Craigslist

Town Hall

Bandit Signs

Real Estate Website

Newspaper Advertising

1. Direct Mail

The advent of technology Has shifted the marketing landscape more and more. Traditional strategy, but this does not mean that those techniques are still not useful. For example, spam is one of the most effective ways to search for land investment properties. There is something about receiving a letter within the mail that people still appreciate. If you have not run an instant mail campaign, there are three main steps to follow: Creating a list of vendors, designing and sending your first letter, and following up to increase your response rate.

Start by getting the simplest possible list of potential vendors for your campaign. A strategic list allows you to focus on those efforts, the qualities you want at the forefront. The lists include pre-foreclosure, probate or inherited assets, expired listings, and state zamindars. Often, these qualities will lead you to motivated sellers who want to sell their homes as soon as possible.

After creating your list of vendors, take the time to style the piece of collateral selling that you will send. It can take the shape of handwritten letters, postcards, and more. Discover options that allow you to send a strong message while staying within your budget.

Once you finalize your list and style, you want to plan to match your pieces continually. Strategize a multi-step campaign and do not hand over any inquiries after the primary mailing. Remember, the response rate will often increase after each additional mail-out!

2. Facebook

Facebook, and for that matter, almost every social media platform, has proven to be quite capable when it involves marketing to a mass audience. This is arguably a user-friendly, cost-effective means of selling to a broad group of users. If you have not yet implemented a Facebook marketing campaign, you are missing a valuable opportunity to secure leads.

To start marketing through Facebook, first, create a page for your business. Fill out your profile by including a corporation description, a link to your website, mission statement, contact information, and even a couple of pictures of your office or logo. This can help users understand what you are doing and can also explain how to get in touch with you. To start generating through Facebook, you will post articles and other useful information in your feed to grow following in your market and interact with other land investors.

3. Other land professionals

It is easy to see other land investors as competing, especially within your market area. However, I always encourage investors to consider other like-minded professionals as valuable contacts rather than competitors. Everyone you contact is usually either a potential lead or a source of referral. Keep this in mind when networking because you never know who your next deal could be. That said, is it best to network with your later contacts:

Other investors: As you already know, as an investor, it is impossible to acquire every deal that comes your way. By networking with other investors, you will position yourself to acquire assets that they will not be able to command. Even you will get opportunities to enter an enterprise. Do your best to build a strong relationship with your fellow investors, and your efforts may be rewarded at some point.

Real Estate Agents and Mortgage Brokers: I highly recommend establishing a solid relationship with both land agents and brokers. They are often the primary people to know when a property becomes purchasable, making it a potential asset for any investor.

Attorneys: Lawyers are regularly hired to represent individuals who may be required to sell their property for any reason: pre-foreclosure, bankruptcy, probate, expulsion, and divorce. Regardless of the case that may happen, they are a natural source who asks about the homes that they are hitting the market.

Contractor: Whenever you work on a project, you should be networking with contractors. Eventually, they are first aware of other land projects taking place within the area. Whether you continuously work with an equivalent contractor or stand in multiple lines, you should aim to build a positive relationship. Not only can they contribute to any current deals, but they will also be ready to point you to your next people.

While these four sources can help you find land deals very easily, they are by no means the only people you should know. Consider someone with connections to the construction industry to be a viable source for land construction. You want to continually make efforts to cultivate relationships with title agents, insurance agents, hard-money lenders, plant department officials, and even friends or relations.

4.Driving

It also happens to be one of the easiest ways to look for deals for the dollar: driving for the dollar. All you can get is a car, a notebook, and a touch effort. Just move around your area and look for homes that want to work or are in the market for extended periods of your time. Properties with overgrown bushes, debris within the yard, and a generally muddy appearance are signs that homeowners may have run out of cash to make improvements and should be looking to sell.

Also, write the address as a property outline as you see potential leads (but not when you are driving). If you are feeling ready, you will try to knock on the door to start a conversation. Tell the owner that you are an investor shopping for homes in the area. Only leave them with your contact information when they know someone curious about selling. After getting a list of your potential assets, add addresses to your spam campaign. All it takes is a keen house owner to show up in a reliable deal.

5. Craigslist

Craigslist has long been a source for landlords and land investors. Look for properties for rent near your area and reach out to Libra landlords - you never know who is eager to sell. An alternative option with Craigslist is to look for property purchases. This allows you to succeed in life as a property owner and find potential investments.

When it includes Craigslist, it is essential to check the listing regularly and follow up with contacts when necessary. The web site is understood for its core competence, not its simple communication. If you have not heard back from Billboard, do not be afraid to send another message with your contact information, Putting the ball in the seller's court.

Remember, the more people you contact, the more likely you are to find someone who is interested.

6. A Town Hall

Much information is available in any government building or courtyard. A good amount of information is available, including eviction notices, probate listings, tax liens, and other tax records. Once you collect specific contact information, you will either send a letter to the property owners, call them, or perhaps play at their door. In these cases, you identify the knowledge you are acquiring from a reliable source, so it is merely a matter of getting their attention and closing the deal.

7. Bandit Signs

Bandit Signs are 18 x 24 signs that you can see in popular city areas or significant intersections. What makes marketing such a great strategy is that you can buy an external quantity of signs for a relatively low price.

The opposite advantage of this strategy is that you only have complete control over the signal, and therefore less information written on the sign is usually the most effective. This is because the

119

people driving these signals do not have time to process such information, whether they are at a stop sign or light. A simple message "we buy houses" or "quick, cash-off" with a telephone number is all it takes.

The key to an honest bandit signature campaign is targeting specific neighborhoods or high traffic areas. Recognize that some cities will ban where you sign, so it is essential to look together with your government before posting anything. Overall, bandit symptoms are usually worth some time and resources.

8. Land websites sites

These are excellent ways to search for Redfin, Zillow, and Trulia. These potential deals may require some digging, but they are for you. Search through rental or buyable posts that have been active for extended periods of your time. In cases of rental units, landlords may not actively try to sell, but they may be hospitable to a reasonable offer. If they are having trouble renting, this may give you a chance to shop. You will also specialize in positions from vendors without land agents. These people could also try for faster transactions.

To make the simplest use of land websites, be prepared to succeed via email or phone, and do not stop after just one attempt. Try testing various messages to find out what an outstanding response rate is and plan your follow-up efforts. Once you find an honest system, the method will not take you a few minutes per day. If you get a single deal from your efforts, it will be worthwhile. Among all available websites, you should find yourself with a minimum of two results to work.

9. Newspaper advertising

It was not that way back that newspapers were a source for anyone to buy, sell, or rent land. In recent years, the recognition of newspaper advertisements has diminished, although this does not mean that they are entirely meaningless. The newspaper is virtually an excellent niche when it involves lead generation, as many investors in your area are ignoring these advertisements.

Reach anyone who lists the property for rent or is selling on their own. The way you approach other leads, prepare as you are saying, and always include your contact information so that they can follow-up. Additionally, understand that it is rare to resolve all from your initial phone. When it includes newspaper advertisements, you often need to reach out multiple times to get feedback.

Find Land Deals with Proper Mindset

Real estate investment involves time, energy, and money; and the small question presents constraints from time to time. It is important not to lose your fire. If you are having trouble finding a land deal right away, do not let it discourage you from your goals. Instead, reflect on why you started investing in land and push yourself to pursue it. The key to future success as an investor is knowing how important your mindset is and how to stay on target.

The first thing you want to understand is that every investor will go through a drought phase at some point. If (or when) this happens to you, it is not a sign that you are simply a failure, but rather a sign that it is time to do something different. An excellent thank you for realizing your vision during this point is to read through success stories on well-known entrepreneurs and investors. Look for situations where they struggled and the way they worked to beat those odds. Often, these lessons apply to your current situation and can help you travel after new deals.

Another way to increase your mindset is the need of the hour and to evaluate your business. There is no need to be afraid of the need for better scrutiny from an old marketing strategy to find out what made it fail. By doing this, you will point out what has gone wrong and prevent yourself from making equivalent mistakes. This process is called refining and will be essential to the success of your future endeavors. Remember that trial and error is a crucial part of marketing, and lead generation is some of the things that you will continuously improve. If you know how to increase past mistakes and maintain a positive mindset while doing so, there is no reason why you cannot achieve success in the future.

Consider buying a property offered by a bank.

When someone fails to pay your mortgage payment for an extended period, the lender will eventually resell the home and take the occupants away. Once the house is vacant, the lender typically employs a local land to list the house's purchasable inventory on the market.

While foreclosure is truly tragic (no one rejoices when they lose a home), once the work is done, these properties are often among the simplest deals you can find in the land. Banks tend to stay within the lending money business, not managing the property, in the order that they often supply large discounts to urge their books to deal with. Translation: If you correctly identify how to buy a foreclosure, you will get an excellent deal on foreclosure properties.

Because the foreclosure process can take many years, these properties often require some severe repairs or updates. Therefore, buyers wishing to brave rehab may be given further discounts to compensate.

Talk to a field land agent about the foreclosure in your area and start investigating some. You will probably be surprised by the deals.

Be primary or last

In the land, often the old saying is true: the first bird gets the worm.

Often, this is not the best offer for a property that is accepted; it merely is primary. So, if you are trying to find an excellent deal, hurry about it! Get preapproval from a bank so that you can walk away from any ownership, and your land agent has set you up with an automated email alert informing you of any new property coming into the market.

Then, do not delay - check it quickly, and suggest an equivalent day if possible.

In contrast, looking for different deals means looking for different properties that are on the market for an extended time. Those owners are often much more willing to sell for deductions, as they are indifferent to occupying the property. Again, and again, they are going to make two mortgage payments for months (or years) and entertain almost any offer.

Privately approach absentee owners

In a hot land market, like most of us are experiencing today, it is often difficult to find, mainly due to the sheer number of individuals trying to find a home. In some areas, a dozen or more offers can be found within the first several days upon purchasing a house.

Therefore, one of the simplest strategies land investors use today seems to be outside of your many listing services and instead contact the owners directly, asking them to think about selling. At any given time, an honest percentage of the population will entertain that option, so why not arrive before listing the house with a real estate agent?

The simplest type of focus on people is one of the absentee owners, which simply means someone who owns the property, but does not live there. They can be landlords (who hate their tenants) or owners who inherit their homes and are simply unsure of what to try with them. You will get these deals in several ways, such as: driving nearby, trying to find empty-looking homes, and using online public records for the owner of a buy, a public records list total-listing such as a list.

To use Mod -and

To use Mod and-Pop Calling landlords who are listing property "for rent" on Craigslist. Allow them to know that you are not curious about renting, but you want to ask them about buying.

Look at tons of deals.

Finally, realize that finding good deals is essentially a "game of numbers." You need to kiss a ton of regular frog prince hunts!

For me, I check deals in terms of funnels. On top of that, there are many leads available, but at Rock Bottom, only a few starts. So, if I would like to do more deals on Rock Bottom, I would like to enhance every aspect of my funnel, with the highest number of standards and leads. For example, my horn might look like the following:

Raw is from my land agent - 200

Where I can buy the location - 100

A quick analysis shows promise - 20

Deeper research still shows promise - 10

Deals suggested -8

The proposition is created that accepts - 1

Notice that above, the funnel 'gemmy agent had sent me 200 potential properties, but at the top, I cave Eight and ended up just making an accepted offer. If I wanted to shop for two yards, I know I would need to be reminded of my funnel and know how to increase my numbers. Because, again, this is just a number pool.

Whether you are shopping for an investment property, buying a house for yourself, or buying land for any additional reason, remember you make your money after purchasing.

If you want to have immediate equity in your property, which can help you build wealth within the future, or just stop in case of financial tightness, then you want to find great land deals.

CHAPTER 7
Set your time.

Real estate agents help people through the method of selling, renting land, homes, offices, and other properties. In addition to staying current with land regulations and trends, land agents are tasked with closing homes and property, from lead generation and marketing to a mess of daily duties and responsibilities.

One of the fascinating aspects of working as a reliable realtor is that every day is different and respond to the changing needs of buyers and sellers often means gear shifts at the eleventh hour. Although a day is exclusive, certain activities would be typical during a day in the lifetime of a reliable realtor.

Administrative duties

On any given day, many activities of one agent are going to be income-producing, while others are going to be strictly administrative. Administrative responsibilities include tasks such as:

- COMPLETING, SUBMITTING AND FILING LAND DOCUMENTS, AGREEMENTS AND LEASE RECORDS,

- COORDINATING APPOINTMENTS, DEMONSTRATIONS, OPEN HOUSES AND MEETINGS, BUILDING AND DISTRIBUTING PASSENGERS, NEWSPAPERS, LISTS, AND OTHER PROMOTIONAL MATERIAL

- CREATING AND IMPLEMENTING PAPER AND ELECTRONIC SYSTEMS FOR RECORDS, CORRESPONDENCE, AND OTHER MATERIALS

- MONTHLY, QUARTERLY AND YEARLY BUDGETING FOR OPERATIONS

- DATA ENTRY

- DEVELOPING MARKETING PLANS FOR LISTINGS

- DEVELOPING AND MANAGING CLIENT DATABASES

- COMPARATIVE MARKETING RESEARCH (CMA) REPORTS RESEARCHING ACTIVE, PENDING AND UNSOLD LISTS

- RESPONDING TO EMAILS AND PHONE CALLS

- UPDATING WEBSITES AND SOCIAL MEDIA PROFILES

- BECAUSE ADMINISTRATIVE DUTIES OFTEN TAKE MUCH TIME, MANY AGENTS EMPLOY AN ASSISTANT TO HANDLE THESE DAY TO DAY TASKS. THIS ENABLES THE AGENT TO LEVERAGE HIS TIME MORE EFFECTIVELY AND, ULTIMATELY, BE MORE PRODUCTIVE.

The lead generation

Finding a client is central to the success of a reliable estate agent; Without buyers and sellers, there would be no transaction and hence, no commission. A well-liked thank you for doing this is through a dedicated property area of influence (SOI) strategy that focuses on generating through people the agent already knows, such as family, friends, neighbors, classmates, business associates, and social contacts.

Because most people will sell, buy, or rent property at some point in their life, each agent can be a potential customer. This means that a dedicated estate agent's day often involves meeting and speaking with multiple people, giving business cards, and keeping track of contact information for a growing network. Meeting people and handing over business cards, however, is only one step in cultivating new leads.

Once primary contact is made, it is vital to periodically follow phone calls, emails, mail, or text messaging to stay fresh in the minds of all potential customers.

Working with customers

Whether performing on behalf of buyers or sellers, land agents usually spend time every day working directly with customers. For example, a seller's agent may spend time preparing an inventory presentation, taking digital photos of the property, and staging the home so that it is well visible. A buyer's agent, on the other hand, can take time to comb through the MLS to print, or email the listing to potential buyers and show the property to interested buyers. Land agents are involved in conducting inspections with customers, meetings with loan officers, terminations, and other activities where their presence is required or requested.

Meeting and Tours real estate agents work under the umbrella of designated brokers and usually operate out of an office with other land agents and brokers. Regular office meetings can help agents share their new listings, update other agents on price reductions, and discuss buyers' needs, and line up agents and buyers and sellers.

Some agents participate in MLS tours to see a variety of the latest lists. This will help agents narrow down the eye for the buyer as they have seen the property for the first time and can share detailed information with buyers. Similarly, MLS tours are often beneficial for agents who are working with sellers. After watching the competition, it becomes easy to work on an honest listing price for the seller's property.

Continuing education and certifications

An actual realtor must be licensed within the state during which he operates and must earn continuing education credits to take care of active license status. Also, for those requirements, most agents follow land certificates and designations to increase their credibility and marketability. Although earning and maintaining licenses, certifications, and assignments will not be the neighborhood of an agent's daily schedule, it is a part of the plan of many agents to improve their skills, competencies, knowledge, and marketability.

Here are seven ways to lean, mean selling machines that require the dog to go to the park or spend weekends within the mountains.

Prioritize Your Daily Tasks with the Eisenhower Matrix

Before you start working smarter rather than harder, you need to sit down and figure out which tasks are absolute priorities, which are essential but not influential., And which tasks are directly wasting time.

Like most great ideas, using the Eisenhower matrix is amazingly simple. Make a list of all the vital property functions that you simply do day to day, and put them all in one of four categories:

1. First,

These should be the main tasks that directly direct you to cold calling, door knocking such as Make

Money, Manage Facebook Ads, and React to New Leads and Current Customers.

As the category name suggests, you should do these tasks first. Joshua suggests blocking the time in your day to urge you to do these tasks. More on this later.

2. Schedule

Significant, but not immediate, you should schedule tasks such as researching replacement CRM, networking with listing agents, optimizing your website, and fragmenting your leads.

3. The rep

Here is where it will be a bit tricky for some agents. If you have help available, it is excellent to do representative work. If not, we have great suggestions to find out. Are you able to delegate social media? Looking for an email address? Screening goes cold.

4. Do not do these tasks that are not helping you in the least. For many people, these are going to be related to social media. For example, have you ever spent an hour each day on Pinterest for six months, with nothing to do for it? Maybe time for a replacement strategy.

Once you do your Eisenhower Matrix, you are likely to scratch your head.

Is it working?

Is it possible to work as a top producer 40 hours per week?

Yes. Yes, and yes.

Here are some recommendations on how you would do it:

Automate outreach and lead nutrition with an honest CRM

Want a secret to land success? Most agents at the highest are quite cheating

No, they are (probably) not violating RESPA or accumulating pocket listings. However, they are using robots to Automate many tasks for what you are probably still doing bizarrely.

Their secret robotic weapon?

A good CRM that helps you reach the appropriate leads at the right time with the right message.

Right now, you might be screaming with Excel, but what happens once you have as many results as 5x?

How are you getting to remember all their birthdays, anniversaries, dates, preferences?

Chances are, you are not.

You are just getting to move forward and letting leads, deals, and, most importantly, potential future referrals slip through various cracks in your system.

A great CRM can prevent the loss of labor per day and help nurture you for longer to become customers and closed deals.

Real Estate CRM

Perfect for small teams and brokerages, Property Base Rock Solid Industry Standard can be a land CRM built on the Salesforce platform.

It offers lots of automation and customization options and offers something that a lot of land CRM does not: it integrates directly with your MLS.

This means you save the assets you like, sending new listings, weekly updates, and Blast with everything you do in your CRM and regular old emails.

Another option would be to check and defeat an IDX website that comes with an integrated CRM. If you are handling many website leads, this may be your best bet.

Good choices here include Real Geeks, Boomtown, and Chaim.

The only downside here is that these systems can be priced quickly.

For an honest IDX website with CRM, you are looking at a bare minimum of $ 150 - $ 250 per month. More sophisticated sites and CRM can cost $ 1000 more per month.

Hire a virtual foreign assistant

This will be out of the "representative" section of an Eisenhower matrix.

Since not every agent can swing a US-based assistant full-time, hiring a foreigner is usually an excellent start.

Many large brokerages and other companies appoint foreign exchange assistants for overseas functions such as listing, updating social media, obtaining contact information, qualifying leads, appointment scheduling, and more.

Here in close, we have given particularly good results from onlinejobs.ph from VA's Philippines. Like India, remote workers within the Philippines speak superb English and even experience a lot of distinctive lands.

You can hire part-time or full-time workers and browse worker profiles to find the right match for your budget and specific workflow.

You can expect to pay anywhere from $ 5 to $ 10 per hour for a professional and hard-working virtual assistant within the Philippines.

Rent an ISA

If it is one of your pain points, giving you cold leads, and if nurturing happens, you probably want to hire an ISA (Inbound Sales Associate).

An ISA does many sales tasks that you can usually do, but the screen is qualified by you so that you can simply find yourself with the cream of the crop.

After this, a schedule can be found to call the ISA and help nurture the cold clues for which you do not have enough time to be above your mind.

While ISAS is often a tremendous benefit for your team, limit the extent to which in many countries, they must be licensed.

This means higher salaries and more difficulty in hiring and retaining talent for brand new and fresh agents.

Instead of browsing the method of hiring your own ISA and you would expect them to spend and have enough work to keep them busy, you might want to think about a service like Agentology.

Agentology provides 24/7 lead qualification and support from its US-based ISA team.

Even better, they charge a reasonable flat rate of $ 25 per month and $ 6 per lead.

Starting a team

If there is one thing that I have learned in almost a decade of working on the ground, involved is that no realtor is an island.

Or, to use a good cheesier cliché, it takes a village to sell several houses.

Think about it. Does the top production realtor know that there is not an assistant, an ISA, a closing coordinator, and a couple of junior agents?

Does the mega top producing agent not have dozens of junior agents if they do not have their broker brokerage?

The answer is almost none.

There is a particularly good reason for that. Teams allow team leaders to delegate.

This means that they will work on small parts of the business that they are great at, like pitching homeowners, or negotiating a deal, while a whole crew of people works on what they are not great at.

If you want to insist further on the land, start a team.

If you want to figure in the ground, but have a lot of leads, many supports, and extraordinarily little chaos, join a team.

Although the parable of superhero solo agents may continue, they are rarer than unicorns in today's tech-driven market.

Spend more on lead generation.

This one-touch counter may seem intuitive, but it will eventually click if you internalize another cliché (the previous one, I promise).

It takes money to make money.

In a way, success in the land is not much more complicated than that.

The more you (smartly) spend on lead generation, the more leads you get, and therefore the more deals you make.

The more deals you close, the more referrals you get.

Rinse, repeat, and head straight to the vacation property in Malibu you have dreamed of.

Indeed, this strategy will leave you with many cookies that fall on the cracks.

Luckily, when you started getting more leads and closing more deals, you used many of the strategies mentioned above to keep your workload out of the constant panic mode you are doing right now.

By the way, did you recognize that 70% of sellers interviewed only one agent before listing their home? If you like sellers (or good buyers for that matter), you might want to urge them as soon as they start their search.

Use time strategically

Another important step towards working fewer hours per week, sometimes more productively.

In practice, it suggests that you may want to adopt two strategies that are proven to increase productivity for many people; time is blocked, and hence the Pomodoro technique.

Let us start with time blocking.

Time blocking

Time blocking is just what it sounds. Rather than sitting at your desk and attacking 1,000,000 small tasks directly, you spend the bulk of your time off and tackle one at a time.

This guarantees that you will be more focused and, thus, more productive.

Suppose you have identified cold calling to determine your essential functions.

Instead of punching calls throughout the day, say two hours each morning to line up separately for cold calling.

Keep doing this until your entire week is blocked, so you are spending the most crucial time just focusing on your most important tasks.

Do let not your program become tyrannical.

The fastest way to throwing your schedule out the window is to show it in tyranny and never, never get distracted by it.

It will be tough. Your days and moods will change. Consider your schedule more of a strong suggestion rather than a command.

Remember Time for rest.

To schedule, Another way to leave your new program is to overbook yourself with work.

Instead, remember to schedule on time to grab a coffee, talk with colleagues about anything that is not grounded, or just go for a walk.

The best thanks for resting in your schedule is to use something called the Pomodoro technique.

The Pomodoro technique

This is used for tomato-sized timers, which the inventor of the system operates, the Pomodoro technique can be simpler thanks to some time blocks to increase productivity.

The idea is that your brain can specialize in a task without wandering for only an hour.

This means that getting up and taking a fast break almost every hour then returning to your work will make you more productive.

Although the evidence for increased productivity is real, a 2014 study of workers found that the highest tenth of productivity employees took a 17-minute break every 52 minutes.

To find this out, you will want to line up a timer with a light alarm set so that you need an opportunity.

CHAPTER 8
Real Estate Investment Tips

Consider your level of comfort with being a landlord

Do you know your way around a toolbox? How are you repairing the drywall or not having to open the toilet? Sure, you will ask someone to try to do it for you, but that will affect your profits. Property owners who own one or two houses often do their repairs to save much money.

Of course, this changes as you add more properties to your portfolio. Lawrence Pereira, president of King Harbor Wealth Management in Redondo Beach, California, lives on the West Coast but owns property on the East Coast. As someone who is not in the least bit of work, he works. How? "I put together a solid team of scavengers, apprentices, and contractors," Pereira states.

Pay down personal debt

Savvy investors can take loans as part of their investment portfolio, but the specific person should avoid it. If you have student loans, unpaid medical bills, or children who will soon attend college, purchasing rental property may not be the appropriate step.

Pereira agrees that it is crucial to be vigilant, stating that "it is not necessary to pay the debt if your return from your land is larger than the value of the loan. This is the calculation you want to make." Pereira suggests that there should be a cash cushion. "Don't put yourself in a situation where you have a shortage of cash to pay on your loan. Always have a margin of safety."

Secure a deposit

Investment properties typically require a larger deposit than owner-authorized properties; they require stringent approval. Three is not working for an investment property you have put at home where you currently live. You will need a minimum 20% deposit unless mortgage insurance is available on rental properties. You will be ready to receive deposits through bank financing like a personal loan.

Find the appropriate location

The last item you like is to be damned with a rental property in the neighborhood that is receding instead of static or learning steam. A city or place where the population is growing and plans for revitalization is underway potentially represented an investment opportunity.

When you choose a profitable rental property, you should look for a location with low property taxes, an honest administrative district, and many amenities such as parks, malls, restaurants, and movie theaters. Additionally, a region with low crime rates and a growing employment market can mean a large pool of potential renters.

Buying with Financing Compare, is it better to shop with cash or finance your investment property? It depends on your investment goals. Cash payments can generate positive monthly income. Take a rental property that costs $ 100,000 to buy. With income, taxes, depreciation, and taxes, the cash buyer could see $ 9,500 in annual earnings.

Conversely, funding can give you more leverage. For an investor who puts 20% down on the house, with a cost of four percent on the mortgage, after removing operating expenses and additional interest, earnings add up to about $ 5,580 per year. Income is lower for the investor, but their annual return on investment is 27.9% versus 9.5% for the cash buyer.

Beware of high-interest rates.

The cost of borrowing money in 2020 may be relatively inexpensive, but the interest rate on an investment property is going to be above standard mortgage interest rates. If you plan to finance your purchase, you will want a coffee mortgage payment that will not increase your monthly profits too much.

Calculate your margins

Wall Street firms that buy distressed properties aim for returns of fifty to seven percent because they need to pay employees. Individuals should set a target of ten percent.

Estimated maintenance costs at one percent of the property's value annually. Other prices include homeowner's insurance, prospective homeowners' fees, property taxes, and monthly expenses such as pest control and landscaping.

Invest in Landlord Insurance

Protect your new investment. Also, consider homeowners' insurance, and consider buying landlord insurance. This type of insurance typically covers property damage, lost income, and liability protection, only due to an injury caused to a tenant or visitor, causing harm to the property—maintenance issue.

To reduce your costs, check if the insurance provider will allow you to ensure the landlord with a homeowner's policy.

Factor in unexpected costs

It is not just maintenance and maintenance costs that will reduce your income. For an emergency, there is always the possibility of roof damage caused by a storm, for example, or burst pipes that destroy the kitchen floor. Decide to set aside 20% to 30% of your income for all those costs so that you can get a fund for timely repairs.

Avoid a fixer upper.

It seems for the house that you can get on just a bargain, and it is tempting to flip into a rental property. However, if it is your first property, it is probably a bad idea. Unless you find a contractor, who does quality work on the cheap - or you are proficient for large-scale home improvements - you are likely to pay an exorbitant amount for renovations. Instead, shop for a home that is priced below the market and only wishes for minor repairs.

Calculate Operating Expenses

Operating expenses on your new property are going to be between 35% and 80% of your gross operating income. If you charge $ 1,500 for rent and your expenses are available at $ 600 per month, you are at 40% for operating expenses. For a simple, easy calculation, use the five hundred rules. If the rent you charge is $ 2,000 per month, expect to pay $ 1,000 in total expenses.

Determine your return for every dollar that you invest, what is your return? Stocks can offer 7.5% cash-on-cash returns, while bonds can pay 4.5%. A six percent return in your first year as a landlord is considered, especially as the number should increase over time.

Buy low-cost homes

Expensive homes are going to be your up-front expenses. Some experts recommend starting in the $ 150,000 range in an up and coming neighborhood. Additionally, experts recommend not to shop for the best home purchase on the block, ditto for the worst house on the block.

They're legal

Owners of rules must negotiate landlord-tenant laws in their state and location. For example, it is essential to know about your tenants' rights and security deposits, lease requirements, eviction rules, reasonable accommodation, and your obligations to avoid legal hurdles.

Weighing the risks versus rewards

Every financial decision is about weighing the rewards, determining the payoff against the potential weight. Do you have to invest inland?

Reward:

Your income is passive. Apart from the initial investment and maintenance costs, you will earn money by spending most of your time and energy in your regular work.

Your income should increase. You do not just earn rental income. If the value of the land rises, then your investment increases in value.

You can land in a self-directed IRA.

Your income is not included as a part of payment under the Social Security tax.

The interest you pay on an investment property loan is tax-deductible.

In another crisis, the value of land is more stable than the stock exchange.

Immovable property can be a physical asset. Investing in stocks or Wall Street products is nothing you will see or touch.

Risk:

Although income is passive, it is often a pain to influence tenants unless you have hired a property management company.

If your adjusted gross income (AGI) is above $ 200,000 (single) or $ 250,000 (jointly married), you will be subject to a 3.8% surcharge on total investment income, including income.

Rental income may not cover the entire mortgage.

Unlike stocks, you cannot sell land immediately if the market turns sour; otherwise, you need cash.

Entry and exit costs are often high.

If you do not have a tenant, you will have to pay for all the expenses.

Take the view that real estate investors should determine their land activities as a business to set short- and long-term goals. A business plan also allows investors to see the bigger picture, which helps them specialize in dreams rather than any minor failures. Land investment is often complex and demanding, and a sound plan can keep investors organized and on task.

Market influential land investors gain in-depth knowledge of their selected market (s). Considering the current trends, including any change in consumer spending habits, mortgage rates, and therefore the percentage, of which a couple has to call, land investors will have to accept the current circumstances and for the long term allows planning. This allows them to predict when the trend may change, creating potential opportunities for the ready investor.

To be honest real estate investors are generally not obliged to maintain a specific degree of ethics.

While it may be easy to take advantage of this example, most successful land investors have high ethical standards. Since land investment involves people, the reputation of an investor is probably going to be far-reaching. Influential land investors find that it is best to be fair, rather than figuring out whom they will avoid.

A separate segment

Develop investors must develop attention to realize the depth of data needed to become successful. Taking time to build this level of understanding of the chosen field is integral to long-term success. Once a specific market is mastered, the investor can progress into additional sectors using a similar depth approach.

Encourage Referral generates a large part of a dedicated property investor's business, so it is essential that investors treat others with respect. This includes business partners, associates, customers, tenants, and anyone with whom the investor accounts. Influential land investors listen to and respond to complaints and concerns in detail and represent their businesses positively and professionally. It builds the kind of reputation that makes others curious about working with those investors.

Be Educated

As with any business, it is imperative to keep up with the laws, regulations, terminology, and trends that make up the business idea of a critical property investor. Investors who fall behind risk losing not only their businesses but also legal hurdles if laws are ignored or broken. Successful land investors are educated and adapt to any regulatory changes or economic trends.

Risk that

Stock or future exchange investors have been flooded with warnings about the risks inherent in investing. Land investors, however, are more likely to detect advertisements claiming the exact opposite. It is easier to make money in the land. Prudent land investors understand the risks - not only in the context of land deals but also include legal implications - and adjust their businesses to reverse these risks.

An account consists of investing a large portion of the annual expenses of a dedicated property investor. Understanding current tax laws are often complex and take time away from the business. Sharp land investors retain the services of a professional, reputable accountant to handle business books. Accountant-related values are often salvable, which may be negligible compared to savings experts.

To get help.

Learn how. Learning a critical property investment business is challenging for someone who tries to do things on their own. Influential land investors often give a portion of their success to others, whether it is a custodian, a lawyer, or a supportive friend. In dealing with a difficult problem rather than risk time and money, successful land investors realize that it is worth the extra cost (in terms of cash and arrogance) to embrace other people's expertise.

Build a network can provide significant support and create opportunities for both new and experienced land investors. Such a group, composed of a well-chosen patron, business partners, customers, or members of a non-profit organization, allows investors to challenge and support each other. Because most of the land investment depends on experiential learning, savvy land investors understand the importance of building a network.

CHAPTER 9
Inspiration for real estate business.

Inspiration and your ability to dig deeper persists even when everyone tells you to stop or when people stop believing is one of the essential things that sets those apart from startup history. Let us complete the pages. Your day of inspiration in the outing has a direct impact on all the latter, just to call something: enrolling others: I often refer to it as a teacher. Among the keys to achieving things, especially things that are difficult, is sharing your goals with others. Once you share your goals with others, not only do you make them curious and excited about what you're doing (because, if they care about you, they want you to succeed), But you can include them in your journey as passengers. Some people can also tell you how things are going and how much progress you are making. The more motivated you are, the better you urge people to be excited about your journey and, if you are lucky, get them to join or help you. Having a team of people around you is often even more critical. When people see the founder as incredibly motivated and feel that energy, it is easy for them to insist on inspiration and to barge in when it gets tough.

Gaining Speed: Have you ever felt that once you do a series of things in relatively quick succession, they repeat over each other? Motivation, and having the ability to dig deep once needed, can be an essential point in building momentum. The faster you, and the people around you, see things happening, the better it is to keep moving forward when things start getting tough. Once you build momentum and see progress, you get into a flow where things just start happening. This often happens when you hire new people in your company. Getting them can be necessary forever and can be a true grind, but once they come in and start delivering things, you will see that things begin to happen, which you are also conscious of. Building a better product: When your motivation level is high, you will be more focused on spending your product at the right time. You will work hard to fix flaws, bugs, or quality issues, which will differentiate between an honest product and an excellent product. You will also inspire others to travel the extra mile to create their products in an innovative way that you do not expect and exceed customer expectations.

Selling more: Your ability to be excited, high energy, enthusiastic, and positive will have an immediate impact on your customers' shopping desire. Once you make that extra sale and get a replacement customer, it also helps build momentum and can lead you to later customers. Just last week, I sold three offers to customers in a row. The energy was contagious, and each sale became easier and more manageable. Customers could feel my energy and inspiration, making it easier for them to connect with me. Motivation leads to success, which boosts your confidence and leads to more success.

Being curious: I often find that highly motivated people are also generally incredibly interested. They are always trying to find ways to disrupt the mold and rewrite the principles of the game. The curiosity is the lifetime of any successful business. It helps us to create better products, gives less time to plug-in, resolves customer issues more quickly, tries out new things, and how to continuously grow our businesses. When you are highly motivated, you are more likely to challenge yourself. Think outside the box to find complex problems.

Find Your Purpose: Until you recognize how you can reach your destination? One of the key accessories that you find among phenomenally successful people, whether they are founders, athletes, or celebrities, can be a crystal-clear sense of purpose. For some, these are some of the most incredible goals, such as treating cancer or winning championships, while for others, their purpose may be to convince themselves and those around them that they will achieve something epic. As a marketing coach, one of the reasons most marketing executives find me is because they are unhappy or frustrated with their lives. They are aimlessly browsing the pace on life's treadmill with no apparent purpose at a time. Once you realize what your purpose is and you share it widely with the planet, the universe just starts clicking on the spot, and it becomes easier to decide what you will and will not do.

Develop smart goals: To accomplish your objective, you will need plans. Once you start keeping your end goals in mind, it is easy to stay motivated as you see yourself progressing. Setting annual, quarterly, monthly, and weekly goals for yourself may seem daunting, and you probably will not always hit them, but it helps you to become disciplined and focused. SMART goals are specific, measurable, accountable, relevant, and time bound. Break those goals down into digestible bits that you can simply work on from day today. The more you see yourself hitting those targets, the better it gets. For example, my annual cycling goal is 2500 miles, so I know I want to ride 208 miles per month or 50 miles per week. More importantly, I share my relationships with Strava with all my followers, which keeps me honest and motivated.

Surround yourself with QOP: Les Brown, who has been considered by many of the world's best motivational speakers simultaneously, it well: Surround yourself with only quality people. The higher-level people surround themselves with you, the more motivated you will feel about pushing yourself beyond your limits, and therefore the more motivated you will be by your success, drive, and eagerness. You will probably also learn a trick or two about how to stay motivated.

Share your goals: It is easy to cheat if you are the only one accountable. If you have found people working with you, especially QOP, then you will use tools like Asanas to create your goals, break them down, and allow others to "accomplish" as you complete them. (or not). Sharing your goals with others not only enables them to help you deliver products but also holds you accountable for acting so that you question yourself about what you do. Let us start trying.

Develop a "killer" routine and live with it: The practice is essential. I cannot insist on it. On average, it takes 14 days to change a habit, but once you get into it, it can make a world of difference. For me, the killer's routine is on my calendar. For example, I say Tuesday typing Tuesday, because every Tuesday I am creating great content.

Here is what my Tuesday routine looks like:

- 6 am and above me!

- 6:15 am 10 mi / 38 min bike ride

- 7:15 am ice cold shower (benefits are great!), Dress, breakfast

- 8:30 am - 9:00 am gratitude magazine / email

- 9am - 10:30 am Podcast creation

- 10: 45am - 12:15 pm Blog post creation

- 12:30 pm - 1:30 pm Lunch with customer, contact or friend

- 1:30 pm - 2pm: 30 am Content Syndication and SEO

- 2:45 pm - 3:30 pm Meeting

- 3:30 pm from school children

- 7:15 pm- 7:15 pm - 5:30 pm Call / Meeting 5:30 pm

-Pm - pm: 00 pm Email / Next day / Presentation time for expenses

- Evening pm: 00 pm Dinner/time with children

- 9:00 pm - 10:00 pm AM Email / Meeting Schedule

- 10:00 AM - 11:00 AM Reading / Meditation

- 11:00 Sleep

You think I try to take a break almost every 90 minutes. At the very least, I try to choose a brisk walk, get some air, stretch, and get some water. Why? Well consistent with this lesson in Fast Company: "Your brain can only concentrate for 90 to 120 minutes before it needs an opportunity. Why? This is the Ultradian rhythm, a cycle that is present both in our sleep and in waking.

Fear Of failure.

Members of the Shark Tank panel write, "No matter what business you're in, you're always in danger - especially in technology, where it changes so fast that you'll have to stay to stay up." "For some 18-year-olds, there is always a chance to come out somewhere and crush you - that inspires me to get out of hell."

"Every single one of my companies, whether I start anything or something I have invested in, can be a scoreboard. How am I doing? Tons of advisors or advisers play it as a number pool."

"If they invest in 20 companies, they recover until success covers 19 losses simultaneously. I check every loss as a massive failure. I recently invested. I lost $ 1.5 million.

It makes me pee non-stop. ".

Failing in something, ask these Mark Cube questions.

"You can also use it as inspiration. What did I do wrong? Whom did I trust that I should not trust? What can I learn from this example so that I can avoid it next time?"

Do what you are passionate about.

That is the key. However, as Chalmers Brown, Co-Founder, and CTO of Dew, writes, "We not only want to make tons of cash but enjoy everything we want. Are. We are willing to take the risk of unstable payments in exchange for following your dreams."

"Unfortunately, your dream job may not always be the simplest decision financially. Sometimes your hobby in your spare time, it is kept as a project for entertainment" (which is excellent!). If you want to venture into showing your passion for a full-time job, the following hints can help you get started properly.

Brown Gives the ideas below:

• Some improvements that you are the first.

• To find out where the market is.

• To share their passion with others.

• Do not be amused and inspired by assigning the tasks that you are not someone else's boyfriend.

Confirm that you go to see.

Online invoicing company Sighted father writes Murray Newlands, "does feel it is straightforward that he was tired or frustrated as an entrepreneur, and sometimes blames you alone." "but a negative attitude mental bandwidth and waste energy Do what you have got to be successful and successful in your life.

"It is essential to take care of an optimistic outlook within the face of failures. Whenever you see a quote or an image that helps you stay positive, keep it front and center so that you remember what this journey."

Take advantage of the rejection facility.

On June 26, 2008, our friend Michael Siebel introduced us to seven prominent people in Silicon Valley. We were attempting to boost $ 150,000 at a valuation of $ 1.5M. That means you would have bought 10 percent for $ 150,000. Airbnb."

You will see five rejections below," Airbnb co-founder Brian Cheeky wrote on Medium. The opposite two were not answered. "The investors who rejected us were smart people, and I'm sure we didn't look imposing. Time."

Surround yourself with extraordinarily successful and motivated people.

During a Q&A in 2016, Mark Zuckerberg said, "Nobody does that." When you examine the biggest things that sweep the planet, they are not done by one person, so you are going to aspire to form a team.

"When building your All-Star team, hunt people who excel in areas where you are not strong, or who have little experience." You need people who have complementary skills, Zuckerberg insisted. "No matter how talented you are, there are just some things that you just don't bring back to the table. "

Never feel sorry for yourself.

"Out of all my successes, everyone had success. There is a failure, so I have learned to look at every belly flopper because something is a good start," said Barbara Corcoran, father of The Corcoran Group and Shark on Shark Tank.

"If you only stick there, you'll find it. Something like this comes true. It is faith that inspires me. I learned never to feel compassion for myself. Just five minutes of realizing yourself take away your power and cause you to be unable to explore later opportunities."

"Look For inspiration.

Motivation can be a drive that you can simply use to inspire you. Lyft co-founder Jordan Zimmerman said, "Right now, my daughter can be a big inspiration. Thinking about the long term of our cities, the planet, and in which environment it is growing old."

Also, the driving force and passenger stories we hear one day. During a previous team meeting, we had a mother available and told the story herself. He may be a Lyft driver living in NY, and his daughter is in LA.

The daughter was browsing a difficult living situation with a roommate and had to move away and enter a replacement location. The mother took her for her daughter. Lyft said, was fast. Interact with the driving force and the driver of his daughter's care in this predicament.

"Ignore your vision.

Yes, believe your eyes. Do not spend too much time on it, or it will knock you down. Elon Musk, for example, spends about half an hour every week. SpaceX's vision of colonization on Mars. Except for those half-hours, Musk focused most of his time on the milestones that are most important, immediate, and important.

Be grateful.

"Most of the time when People ask me with inspiration What can be known as 80 percent of the world. Gary Anarchic writes, "If you want real fuel for victory, you will be grateful.

" Or a brilliant employee, or many dollars in revenue, I default to gratitude. When you are feeling grateful, it is not impossible to stay motivated or get down. "

'You' takes much time.

It is easy and customary to urge you to get lost within the hustle and bustle of building your business. You have got long workdays, replies to messages at all hours of the day, and potential Chase business when it is within your grasp. You recognize it; you start hating your business because it has transcended your life. You will fall in love once. Begin to urge bitterness. To keep you constantly motivated, you will like the break.

You need to set several "your" times. And the hours once you turn off "business mode." Set boundaries with and set aside several times to do things that bring you light. You will want to recharge your batteries so that you can become stronger after the time of "you "not.

Create Connection to Hebdomadally.

Man has struggled in terms of other people. If you build a business on your own will, try, but at some point, you must include others. This is about bringing in employees, a virtual assistant, or a strategic partnership. But also, it is human interaction and connection through groups and masterminds. Do not build your business on an island.

Constant inspiration comes when you are sharing experiences with other motivated people. You learn from each other while a connection is made in your DNA. Keep Mastermind apart, connect, and meet fellow entrepreneurs who can help you on your entrepreneurial journey.

Listen to what great entrepreneurs do that you are working on needing to say to try to get things done.

Once you feel down, hit "play" and get a momentary boost of motivation to go.

A mission is more than just a business.

Look at any successful business, and you will see that it is quite widgets, marketing, or responsible. They are businesses that are built around a mission and vision. There was an expedition which formed the business with the highest goal of assisting the people and transforming the planet.

Constantly and consistently seeking inspiration, once you build your business around an idea that is bigger than just making money. Build a business that makes an impression on the life of these functions of your business, A business that builds independence and financial security. Be clear on your mission and, therefore, the values that shape the work you are doing.

You are an entrepreneur who is building your dream. You are placing your bets during a world that is full of conformity. It will take tons of consistent motivation to cope with adversity as there will be many of them every day. Use these four tips to tap into your inner strength and try to use that inspiration to do amazing things.

Lightning Source UK Ltd.
Milton Keynes UK
UKHW020831151220
375245UK00004B/823